Aspire Aikido

The Budo Classics N. 2

Nick Regnier - Aspire Aikido

Copyright © 2022 The Ran Network

First Edition

Publisher: The Ran Network
info@therannetwork.com
https://therannetwork.com

Cover image: Copyright by Stephanie Belton ©2021

Cover and layout design: Simone Chierchini

ISBN: 9798844531491

Imprint: Independently published on Amazon KDP

Nick Regnier

Aspire Aikido

The Ran Network

Contents

Someone asked me a question: "How do I get my strenght in Aikido?"
I said adopt and follow this: "Fall eight times and get up nine".
This is how you find your strength and determination, not just in Aikido
but in life...

Nick Regnier

Foreword

Tony Sargeant

If you are waiting for something to change without doing anything, nothing will change.

After fifty years of training and forty-seven years of teaching I have many stories to tell, and not all of them have been as enjoyable as connecting with Nick. Our original communication was via social media.

Once we had made that connection we sent many messages and - like most conversations in aikido - the discussions became in-depth.

As time went by, Nick and I discussed our thoughts, we were meticulous and delved deep into the roots of aikido, bouncing views between each other. I had no idea at the time that Nick had suffered from hearing problems all his life; after all, why would one know this as we only talked via email and Messenger, never face-to-face?

Most days I get many emails and correspondence from around the globe. This is because I have got to know many aikidoka due to so many years of following Saito sensei and attending at least two seminars every year. There are many aikido fanatics who desire that regular injection of pure aikido adrenaline that is only achieved through constant training.

Mentioning this leads me to talk about Nick, my journey, and how my thoughts of him have built rapidly over time.

50 years of Aikido training and teaching will be achieved by me in the coming months, my path has crossed hundreds of people from all over the globe. Some lived at my *dojo* as *uchideshi,* which allowed me the privilege to teach and watch their progression; I was able to pass them my understanding of what other great teachers have given to me.

Many went on to become some of the best students and teachers of this wonderful art.

Once these students moved on, they often invited me to visit them in their countries and teach their students. It is an honour for me to experience other cultures and to see how they have advanced in the art of aikido.

When I met Nick I knew he was unique: when he told me of his hearing problems, it made me think back many years to when I was listening to Saito sensei who said, "*The Japanese watch yet, the Westerners question*". Saito sensei talked about his style of teaching which was O-sensei's aikido, he expressed how it was straightforward and clear, "*No words*" were required. On remembering Saito sensei's words, I realised that Nick must have learnt with his eyes which in turn built and advanced his aikido to the heights that it is today. This took Nick many patient years.

After listening to Nick, his thoughts and how he sees and thinks of this special art, it resonated with me how he had been loyal, how he followed so many teachers and humbled himself to what they asked and commanded of him. This is a trait not many can withhold over many years, especially when the mind is collecting so much in-depth information. One can start to question if the information is constructive and the 'truth,' but Nick always persevered. The great Nelson Mandela, even though incarcerated for many years, did not stop his brain from gaining knowledge. I saw this talent in Nick, I wanted to help him become his own master.

Not all prison bars can be seen except by those on the outside.

Imagine seeing what we know is the best racing pigeon but it is locked up in a cage; the message to me is to open the door and let it fly free.

Well, that's what I wanted to do with Nick, and in the last few years, he is flying better than most whom I have seen, taught, or have been acquainted with over my 50 aikido years.

Nick is constantly passing his knowledge to others; all those years of learning are being allowed to flow, he is teaching others to grow and at the same time accomplishing further development in his own aikido ability.

Where the limits are, no one knows. Nick has demonstrated his proficiency in aikido; his written words will help many to understand his passion for aikido and help them to recognise that over many years of hard training, they too can have Nick's high degree of skill and his ability to share knowledge. This will make future aikidoka become the racing pigeons who learn to open their own cage doors to find freedom.

It is a pleasure to write this for Nick's first book, I know the best in Nick is still developing, there is much more to come.

I wish Nick well as I do all those I have been fortunate enough to teach and train alongside.

Many of those whom I meet, no matter which country they come from, say that they wish they had kept training in aikido. Others are overweight and unfit. I often question what they think when looking in the mirror, have they wasted their lives by not keeping their body and mind in fit condition?

Our bodies are made up of so many muscles, tendons, etc. and all require constant active use.

We do not have to choose aikido but, some fitness will always be required throughout our lives; when we look back, can we say that we made the most of it by remaining healthy?

You can never become the people you admire.
You can only be the person you are.

I relate to Nick and hope many of you will too. We are all ordinary people, most have been bringing up a family and, in Nick and my case, also running a large business which entails early starts and very late working nights. We are not heroes, just busy people who work, play and know that if we wish to survive this life in the body that we have been given, it needs to be looked after and not abused week after week, always hoping some magic wand will make it all healthy; sadly it will not and only you, yourself, can protect your body and mind from the harshness of life.

I see Nick's awareness of this, it is not all about his desire and love for aikido: it is also about his vibrant, overflowing enthusiasm and his pure quality passion. This world is in short supply of positive thinking people, I hope you will read Nick's thoughts, his blogs, listen to his films and help yourself to find how to open that cage door that may be holding you back.

Just like you, we do not have any spare time either.

No matter the ageing, time cannot be gauged on how much one can do if let out to fly.

Only at the end of your journey will you know if you followed the correct path.

Tony Sargeant, August 2022

11

Introduction to Aikido

Here is my own intro as to why I joined aikido when I was young: everyone who knows me, is aware of the fact that I have a profound hearing loss and I have been wearing hearing aids from very early age. My mum had rubella when she was pregnant and as a consequence I was born with this disability.

When I became a teenager, I grew with a big interest in martial arts and loved watching martial arts films (chinese kung fu, Jean Claude Van Damme and, yes, Steven Seagal). When I was 15 years old I frequently bought martial arts magazines and even put up posters of Bruce Lee, Jackie Chan and Van Damme in my own bedroom! In secondary school I had a friend who was Vietnamese. He also had an interest in martial arts and was learning kung fu from his dad, who was a kung fu master. I met his dad, who was in his 70s, and he showed me what he was able to do: push ups with two fingers, lifting is legs off the ground and keeping them parallel to the ground – I was impressed! At my age, I could not do what he did. He said that it was *qi*. I asked if he would teach me but he said that he was too old now.

He also said that if he was to do it all over again, he would have chosen aikido. I asked him why. He said in broken French: "Aikido Master is like an egg. No one can truly grab him and he uses the force of his opponent. Aikido is very good". I was intrigued.

So I began searching for a local aikido dojo and found one in Nantes and went to watch a whole session. I immediately fell in love with it: I thought the movements were very gracious and harmonious.

I signed up and began my journey learning aikido. The school belonged to the Aikikai. I even bought a *ken* and a *jo,* although not the Iwama ones

– remember that in France we did not know Iwama Aikido much, so I had no idea it existed. Quickly I realised that as I was a very shy teenager, my confidence was not as high as I would have wanted to be. However, aikido gave me inner strength. I was enjoying the sessions and after each one I quickly became 'hungry' for more. I joined a few aikido seminars when one was held in Nantes.

I grew feeling stronger and more confident because training made me realised that I was able to do the techniques and breakfalls better than some people (who could hear normally). It made me reflect on how it helped me to develop my confidence: thanks to aikido, I felt more ready to take some tasks that I would have thought impossible before, such as taking a phone call. When you wear hearing aids, taking phone calls would be a huge challenge to understand what the caller may be saying. At the time, also, hearing aids were not as advanced as they are today: there would be whistling if the phone got too close to the hearing aid, which would add further complications.

At the age of 20, after studying Hospitality Management, I took on a very different path and travelled to London hoping to learn English. I planned on doing my best to find a good job, and one that would allow me to continue practicing aikido. My first visit to London was in 1991.

I began working in a hotel in Holborn as a waiter. The money was not so great but the job offered a living accommodation with food included and I had a bedsit. During my breaks I was able to study aikido with Minoru Kanetsuka sensei, who was teaching in Euston in two different dojo depending on the days. I was a very keen student but the learning was difficult, as Kanetsuka sensei would often change techniques and I was unable to study in depth any of them.

However, one thing that got me was that Kanetsuka sensei was extremely supple and could almost do the full split in the warm up, so I decided to work on my stretching (which I have been doing regularly to date) and I could notice how much it helped my aikido and my wellbeing.

Then after two years, I decided to take a different direction jobwise and thought I would try and work in the security sector as a Door Supervisor in night clubs. I wanted to earn better money and also, perhaps naively, see how aikido would work...

Before I could work as a Door Supervisor, I had to undertake specific training and do a test to get a licence. I found a training centre in West Hampstead Square with an aikido instructor (Yoshinkan Aikido) named David Rubens. I did my training course and passed all the tests and I was ready to go and quickly got a job in a night club called 'Vogue' in Wardour Street (off Oxford Street).

David asked if I would be interested in joining his class. He had returned from Japan from being an uchideshi for nearly 5 years with Gozo Shioda sensei. He took part into an intensive training course to become instructor and got his 4th Dan in 5 years! I thought this was very quick.

I said OK.

My first class was a shock to me, as he taught his lesson very strictly and I was soon out of breath and thought I was going to die. I managed to pull through and stayed for around two years and earned a brown belt (Yoshinkan use colour belt system).

However, while working as a Door Supervisor in night clubs around that time, there had been occasions when I had to use aikido to defend myself and to escort people off the premises, and there were times when I felt that my techniques did not work as planned.

There was a time when I felt in despair and thought aikido should work, but I thought if aikido did not work properly, it would be because I had not learnt it properly.

My love for aikido was stronger inside me and it helped me to research further. I think if I did not love aikido, I would have given it up then. I went into a book shop and looked at aikido books and luckily I found some books about Morihiro Saito sensei. In one of them he was explaining that "Aikido must be practiced with *bukiwaza* to have a deeper understanding of it and that bukiwaza and *taijutsu* were working together very solidly". I felt in my heart that this was what I had to do.

So I began searching for an Iwama Ryu Aikido club and found The London Aikido Club where met Andy Hathaway sensei. It was back in 1995.

In later years, I also met Tony Sargeant sensei and became a member of the TIAE (Takemusu Iwama Aikido Europe). Tony has been a guide and mentor allowing me to pursue my aikido dream, which is to teach Iwama Aikido preserving the Art that Saito sensei taught us and to help others develop their full potential and more.

5 Steps to Learn and Progress in Aikido

I am listing five steps that have helped me develop my aikido:

1. Put your ego in a box – this means to practice remaining humble and with humility.
2. Learn with beginner's eyes – always be receptive and take in new things you did not know.
3. Practice joyfully – embrace the present or 'now' moment and enjoy feeling the technique whether you are *tori* or *uke* and the interaction with your partner, all with a good heart from within.
4. Practice seriously – aikido is a martial art, so it should be studied thoroughly in every details to get the techniques working. If the technique has failed it isn't because of aikido, it is simply that you have not got the technique correctly.
5. Use your mind, body and spirit when you perform any techniques so that you are completely focused on the movement that you are performing. When you use your mind, body and spirit, you will eventually make the technique become alive and real.

None of these 5 steps is easy. They all require discipline and determination to continue with our own practice through repetition.

To put it simply, we all have a mountain to climb and there are no shortcuts - in aikido like in any martial arts - to get to the top. It is up to us where we wish to climb it but to be absolutely focused, we need a vision or a dream to see where we would like to be. When you have this vision in mind, it can help you push yourself further and who knows you may even be surprised how far you could exceed this vision, a step at a time...

Does Aikido Need Modernising?

I recently noticed (especially since the lockdown) that there are a number of discussions about aikido within our community, in which its effectiveness is questioned or whether aikido needs modernising. This is certainly an interesting topic to address.

Here is my personal view on these discussions.

I do not think aikido needs modernising. The Art that O-sensei left us in the last 10 years of his life was his final aikido, which led to the forming of *aikiken* and *aikijo* with strong taijutsu interlinks. Studying bukiwaza will help any aikidoka to have a sense of increased *zanshin* and awareness of being surrounded, which taijutsu presents in each and every technique - starting with *tai no henko*, for instance.

I do not think the attacks need to be modified. It is all there but the difficult thing for many to understand is that it takes years of practice to do them well and to understand the fundamentals behind these techniques. To me, aikido is complete and very advanced.

There is therefore no need of adding anything new or of simplifying it. If one is struggling with any technique, then it is because you have not yet applied it correctly: the technique is not to blame.

For instance, many techniques will require *atemi, awase* with strong principles of triangle, circle and square. If you take any of one of the above out, the technique will simply fail.

Some discussions extend to even add competitions in aikido. In my view, if we adopt an ideology of winning/losing in our mind because we are competing, we simply deviate away from the spirit aikido is all about.

Indeed, one needs to find the connection and use it to his/her advantage to overcome uke. Breaking his/her balance from start to finish is the ideal aikido to me, and of course doing it by using the right power from the hips and *kokyu* - not the physical muscular added strength to overcome your opponent. If you use the latter and your opponent is stronger, you will simply not succeed, therefore your aikido will have limited effectiveness.

The key is to remain relaxed and adopt the right mindset, which is to connect, reconcile and have the upper hand of the situation as tori, and for uke to feel the technique and learn to know where and when it becomes an effective technique. Adding competition in aikido, would kill this mindset and the ideal connection or blending (awase) that we want to achieve, which takes years of practicing it (I reckon 10 years plus!)

One needs to be very patient and seek to study at one's pace. Unfortunately, after a couple of years often practitioners want to see some strong results. To begin to be good in aikido, however, may take over 10 years at least (if not more). It is a long journey.

However, the journey in learning aikido is a wonderful path and is truly fascinating as no matter how far you go, you will always continuously learn the Art - there is no end goal to it!

If someone is seeking quick results, then aikido is probably not the right martial art. Remember: aikido study (if you are serious about it) is a lifetime commitment.

There are no shortcuts to get to the top and it is up to us, as individuals to find the correct way to apply techniques. We need to be honest with ourselves if we want to truly progress.

However, if you apply correctly all the principles that O-sensei left us, then there is no doubt that in time you will understand them more in depth and that you will then begin to create or innovate aikido following these principles - which I believe is the next level up, called 'Takemusu' Aikido, where one can perform spontaneous techniques from the body (and not the brain) from being exposed to any given situation...

Aikido is a Never Ending Learning Process

After practicing aikido for over 32 years, it would be fair to say that I could give my own view and comments on why I believe aikido is a never-ending learning process. For instance, whenever we think we are beginning to understand a technique or think we know how such technique is performed, often, we quickly realised that we were wrong!

The deeper we study aikido over the years, the quicker we could fall into a trap, especially if we let our Ego dictate us, which is what we, as human beings, constantly tend to do: it's a continous fight against the three biggest vices, such as money, power and sex.

Aikido can only help us if we learn to put our Ego aside. Then, it will begin to forge your body, mind and spirit as one - just like when we practice weapons, we become one with the weapon.

Aikido is not a religion but a deep and advanced martial art that allows us to shape our spirit to be not only physically strong but spiritually better prepared so that we can become better human beings.

When you read the above it may sound quite a cliché. We all know that life is far from easy, and we are all human beings, so we have flaws. Often we hear the wrong inner voice, which tells us we want to be the ruler and be more important than anyone else. This bit does sound a little awful if you attain a deeper understanding of the spiritual world, but it would actually sound fine for many!

The fact is that we are all unique and different human beings but despite this, aikido offers a way to reconcile people and be at peace with one another. To doo this, however, we really need to work on ourselves first!

That is why we keep practicing aikido, we keep going to the dojo over and over again, and we practice repeatedly with different techniques. We do it to learn how to absorb these physical movements that follow very specific principles (triangle, square, circle and spirals), which subconsciously, over the years, gradually affect our spirit for the better, but only if we practice this Art diligently.

There have been times when I felt that the training was amazing, when practicing with a good uke who knew how to respond to all techniques I was performing. It also made me realise that this could be when I least learn aikido! Because uke knows what is going to happen and facilitates it. There could be an illusion where I feel no danger or worst where I believe that my technique works great - until I practice it with a complete novice and the real challenge begins.

Understandably, we feel frustrated and let our ego tell us 'my aikido is not good enough'. This thought would hurt anyone's feeling because we have worked so hard 'to make it work', right? But some techniques are designed to really work after years and years of practice (and not before!) because, they require our body to be using exactly the exact feet and hips positioning, with the right mindset, and feeling of the centre from the belly. The latter is what is truly needed to get it all working but the hard part is that it does take years to acquire the perception of this feeling.

Instead, when we practice our aikido with a novice I can say that we do get this amazing opportunity to test our aikido better. Indeed, we become more ready or alert for the unexpected, therefore we raise our zanshin (which is a good thing), and we learn to practice in a way in which we are prepared for any possible reactions.

Strangely enough, when we feel not so great about practicing certain techniques with a novice, it is when we get to learn aikido at its best because we become conscious of our mistakes! We are 'peeling off a new layer' to understand our aikido deeper...

To progress further, however, one needs to give up his/her ego and remain humble, with a good heart, then it will become possible to advance further in aikido - providing that you have the skills and tools to climb the next higher hill. Sadly, if one is not willing to do this, then his/her aikido will 'stagnate' and not progress much further.

On a deeper level, when we become ready for this, we come to realise that there is a higher level that allows our spiritual growth and this is deeply linked with our life journey and understanding of this Art. It connects us with one another and is filled with compassion (the heart needs to be ready to give).

When we are beginners, we visualise aikido as something that is only very external. We look at the external form, at where your hands should go, at where you are supposed to put your feet. And we think that is all we need to understand.

On the contrary, an experienced aikidoka will begin to see something way beyond hands and feet, and will start to perceive his centre's feeling and with hip movment during very specific techniques (*irimi nage, kote gaeshi, sankyo* etc).

We start to perceive the big and small rotations and spirals, and square and triangle feelings which form our stance beside our feet positioning. We begin to picture the principles behind these forms that we failed to understand when we were beginners.

Writing this chapter made me realise how fascinating this Art is, as it is unlike any other martial arts, where one would be thinking that we practice with an opponent and have to do whatever is necessary to win a fight and bring him down. Sadly, for many winning is important in this world.

A beginner joining aikido, very quickly will find it quite different, as there is no winning or losing concept, which may sound odd. Instead we are all equal. Additionally, we do not treat our uke, the person receiving the technique as an opponent but as a PARTNER. From the very beginning we learn to take responsibility to look after him/her during practice.

Like any other martial art, we also quickly learn to respect one another. A beginner will appreciate this as would anyone else that wish to feel safe and not be part of any 'beating' with one another. In aikido though, the sense of respect really goes much further. Indeed, an experienced aikidoka will sense the need to not only be respectful, but also to connect with his/her partner with awase at a physical level and to feel awase in our heart.

If you watch how Mitsuteru Ueshiba Hombu Dojo-cho bows,[1] you will notice that he does it so precisely, like it is an Art in itself, and he does it in a truly elegant way, and with a good heart. He is beautifully bowing and it is like he is sacrificing his physical body, mind and spirit as one in that very act.

I found that when we practice with a good heart, remaining humble,

---

[1] https://www.youtube.com/watch?v=VpREtleY4FA

we begin to care even more about our partner. There may be a spiritual aspect to this, hence some aikidoka perceive this feeling more deeply than others.

To me, the fact that I practice aikido in a martial way, retaining strong effective aikido techniques (keeping atemi, for instance), helps me to be aware that I practice an aikido that is foremost effective and therefore potentially dangerous. It is the latter, that will make me want to care more about my partner or anyone I practice with.

The same is true outside of the dojo, where we want to find a way to bring peace and avoid having to fistfight to resolve any conflict. Aikido offers all the tools necessary to make us better human beings.

I think it is fair to say that in order to maintain peace (in terms of resolution) one needs to be taken seriously as a martial artist. In that case the 'enemy' would not dare to challenge this martial artist. In my view, peace is preserved because the enemy knows that he is facing someonewho would be too strong to defeat. Therefore he walks away – so to speak.

On the other hand, if the martial artist is not practicing strong aikido, the enemy may be tempted to attack. It is the same situation that we find on the street, where the mugger will carefully choose his victim: the one that is unprepared and unaware of his surrounding.

Now, to feel safe, one does not need to become a complete martial expert. Aikido will quickly help you to become aware of your surrounding and to keep a safe distance. That way, if you are sensing that something is wrong down the street, your gut feeling may warn you, because aikido has taught you to listen to your primary instincts. Aikido will have raised your level of alertness and you will choose to avoid walking on that street and walk away. Aikido can develop this sense of prevention.

I could continue writing more about aikido, that can help many people on so many levels. What I find even more fascinating is that it does connect us with all ages, all nations without any barriers and it does make you feel (if you have a hearing disability like I have) that you can achieve just the same as everyone else, if not more!

So I would just say embrace being a beginner at your own level, like I am a beginner at my own level.

And above all, embrace the fact that we will all remain beginners at our own personal level and that we will endlessly be learning every time we practice. Therefore, I think aikido is magic...

Should Uke Resist Their Partner From Executing a Technique?

If you have never practiced aikido you may not know this, however, this topic is continuously coming back every now and then. I guess we feel differently about it when we study and progress in aikido over a period of time.

What I know for sure, is that any teacher in the dojo will want his new students to perform the technique without feeling too much resistance from uke, so that they can first copy and then perform the technique as best as they can. Otherwise, the training itself could hinder their efforts and enjoyment.

When a beginner has to perform the technique, often uke would be more 'experienced' than his/her partner and would agree to 'let' tori execute the technique while uke is willingly cooperating or 'guiding'.

Nevertheless, I do recognise that this type of training in which uke allows tori to execute the technique can also be a challenge for uke on so many levels. Firstly, for the technique to be strong, uke would want to feel he is losing his power and balance at the right time, thus preventing him from retaliating. The reality is that it would take years of practice for tori to get to this level (as well as years of practice as being uke too!).

As a consequence, uke may be tempted to explain with words in order to help his partner, which is a big temptation for us all, as it is easier to talk than guiding tori without a word and let him lead the technique.

We know that talking prevents good training, as aikido requires the physical movements to be done repeatedly until we begin to assimilate what is happening – so there is a process of doing rather than speaking. Do you remember this? "You hear you forget – you do, you remember".

By practicing in this manner, we begin to feel connected with our primary instincts as well, knowing where and when to block and where to strike, which will help us respond more spontaneously. This is an important part of our training.

In fact, if we look at the way many senior Japanese teachers were teaching, you will find that most of them would use the old Japanese methods of teaching, i.e. the teacher would show the technique a few times without saying any words and let their students practice and find their own way to copy and try and feel the technique. If the students were doing it wrong, often they would not even be shown the right way. The traditional method would rely on the students to find the right way themselves, which would take years. Sadly, some may never find the right way if they have to stop training with a teacher because of injuries or due to a job change or because they have to relocate and so on. The 'no talking' policy, in my view, can take too long to see good result.

If I see a student doing the technique wrong, I would always want to help and show how the technique is done, so I would give a new opportunity for the student to correct his mistake. Then it would be up to them to assimilate and add this good advice to help their aikido.

I have to say that we, the Iwama Aikido community, are extremely fortunate that we had Morihiro Saito sensei who was unique and different from many other Japanese teachers. Morihiro Saito sensei knew how to connect with Westerners and understood them better too by meeting their needs quickly when stuck with any technique. Indeed, Morihiro Saito sensei was able to provide detailed explanation and break the technique down giving pedagogic explanation on why a certain thing was incorrect and why we must practice in a certain way instead.

Since the passing of Morihiro Saito sensei, we are still fortunate to be able to freely watch his videos on YouTube – by the way, thanks to every video owner who knew that they would be treasure to share, rather than keep those videos for themselves. We are very grateful for that!

Morihiro would often say that we should practice *kihon* for some time before we 'jump' into *ki no nagare* and I believe he said that was until one reaches the *sandan* level: That with the goal of building stability and hip power. When we begin in kihon, we allow uke to attack firmly: in other words, **tori is in the worst possible situation to start with**.

The only way to get out of this situation would be to do the technique correctly. But what do I mean by doing the technique correctly? Well, there are quite a lot of points that I would focus my attention on, things that would be very important to me - and some teachers or practitioners may share my point of view or they may take a different approach, which is fine:

1. correct footwork (*hanmi*);
2. correct use of the hips;
3. good posture, upper body staying relaxed, the relative muscles not being tense, connected with hip awareness;
4. feeling the kokyu in your hands and be guided by the movement of your hips, ready to perceive when and where uke is losing power and balance;
5. keeping a good zanshin;
6. practicing with idea in your mind that you are doing bukiwaza when you are practicing taijutsu, so that you retain a strong interlink about how and where you should move;
7. always practicing as you were being surrounded by multiple attackers.

There are lots of things we would need to ensure we do to tick all the boxes, but there is one crucial point: when uke applies lots of power or strength in the grip, for instance, the only way to do overcome this is by staying relaxed, 'centred' and by using hips power. I must say that it is very easy to write it down but it takes many years of practice to get up to this level.

Until then, you will be tempted, like every beginner (and we have all been there, myself included!) to use your arms and shoulders and exert some physical power to subdue your partner, which would work if uke is weaker than you.

Truly speaking, one should be able to practice a strong aikido on someone else bigger than us and the only way to do it is to discover the right use of your hips! Otherwise, your aikido will be fairly limited. If you are big, you could 'make it work' until you meet someone else twice your size...

Now, if an experienced aikidoka performs a technique and uke is still more experienced than tori, I do believe that uke should do what he can to resist when attacking firmly to make tori work on his technique.

However, this is where it becomes tricky.

As teachers, we would need to immediately assess if uke is resisting his partner for the right reasons, for example to help the partner with some resistance for tori to better work on his technique, using his/her hips; or is uke applying more strength than he should because he is driven by his ego to prove the point that he is better and stronger than tori?

The latter would not bring any good feeling to the practice, and it should be avoided at all cost.

Aikido only forges our mind, body and spirit if we rid of our own ego and become humbler. This is something that some practitioners may still have a hard time accepting. We should practice with the former mindset, that is to help our partner in getting a good opportunity to experience resistance (with no vile intention) and to work on their technique using more of the hips and less of the arms, for instance. This engagement becomes extremely productive.

If tori finds it difficult because uke's strong grip is too much to overcome, then uke should lessen the grip a bit allowing tori to continue performing the technique and work on it based on the hip movements.

Only then, after repeated practices, tori would be ready to overcome stronger attacks. Just like when you go to the gym, you would never start with lifting the heaviest weight but you would build on your own strength first and gradually build up your training by lifting.

Aikido has all these traits and amazing abilities to help one another become better and more respectful people. It is through training and the sharing of love for aikido that we manage to achieve truly amazing things afterwards.

Thus, bear this in mind: we need one another to learn this Art, and to practice the right way is the key to progress and build our confidence!

Adopt 'Kaizen' Approach When You Practice Aikido

First of all, you may wonder what is *kaizen* if you have never heard this word before. Well, I never heard this word too until I recently read a book about Toyota[2] (yes, the car manufacturer – as I have a penchant and interest in cars, as some may have noticed). A friend of mine recommended I should read it to help me understand their success and how they became one of the largest car manufacturers in the world - the biggest until the end of 2019, when they were overtaken by Tesla, as a matter of fact.

In this book, the word kaizen did appears quite frequently. It means to seek constant improvement by adopting a certain philosophy and mindset - in their case to improve and make better cars, avoid stocking unnecessarily become extremely efficient in building and assembling all parts to build cars as quickly as possible and sell them fast to meet customer demands.

In the context of aikido, I do believe that the word kaizen is a brilliant one to retain for our learning of the Art: it points out the need to improve our techniques, making them strong and effective, devising how to minimise our footwork to conserve our energy without wasting it pointlessly. It emphasises the performing of a beautiful aikido that catches people's eyes with perfect awase, where we feel a strong connection between tori and uke forms, with no delay between action and reaction - a perfect blend where tori is leading the situation always maintaining the upper hand.

To me, this kaizen approach is very helpful. It is also extremely important, vital, if we wish to deeply improve our aikido.

The reality is that aikido is very difficult to perform and takes years to master. If we focus just on awase for now, we know that this perfect blend

Jeffrey K. Liker: *The Toyota Way: 14 Management Principles from the World's Greatest Manufacturer,* McGraw-Hill Education - 2021 is also equally hard to achieve. We will not manage good awase, that is a good action/reaction mode - for the first few years. Sometimes, we may feel 'yes I have found it' and then we lose a bit of it again; over the years, however, with consistent practice being in awase does sharpen and gets better and better.

To make this even more complicated, the blending with one partner is not just the end goal but the means to be able to move away from a starting point, for you to be in a better situation to deal with multiple attackers.

The kaizen approach remains ever so strong, as you may be asking yourself: 'am I blending enough?' or 'am I moving with my hips strong enough?' or 'am I using my arms?' or 'is my posture affected as a result of my turning or trying to bring my partner down?'

The important thing, as I see it, is to be continuously aware that your aikido is on an evolutionary path or improving continuously, providing that you allow it to progress. If you lose the kaizen approach, then you risk reaching a point where your aikido will stagnate: this will be when you stopped using kaizen or learning the Art with fresh beginner's eyes. Sadly, I have seen some long-term practitioners who have been practicing aikido for years and years and yet their aikido has not vastly improved over these years.

If you are a beginner, you will surely progress with aikido or any other martial art over a period of time by just attending the sessions on a regular basis. You will have the desire to progress – some will progress quicker than others and that is OK, as aikido is not a competitive martial art. You progress at your own pace whenever you can join any session. I would add that when you practice aikido it is important that you should do so feeling happy and enjoying every class you attend - like I have been feeling for over 32 years doing aikido. If you retain this feeling of enjoyment, you will be in your best element to progress.

Thus, to me it is clear that the kaizen approach should always be retained, but especially when you become an advanced aikidoka. Some aikidoka will fall into this common trap (if I may say) that when they reach *shodan* level they may feel that they have achieved and 'mastered' aikido. We all get this feeling after working so hard to get there. I suppose that for a short moment we believe we have become some kind of an expert.

Some may also admit that they had practiced all this far only to get the black belt and sadly choose to 'stop' practicing aikido because their goal was achieved.

To be frank with you, when we become shodan we all feel as if we have climbed a huge mountain, one that appeared impossible to ascend when we first started, only to discover that in aikido and all other martial arts there is always a new mountain being revealed to us. The shodan level is only the beginning to a new level ahead.

This is what motivates me, to know that there is an unlimited way to progress and it is up to me how far I wish to go. To best describe how I live with aikido, I believe it is identical to brushing my teeth in the morning and evening daily. If you want to keep your teeth in good health, you have to brush them. To keep things relatively simple, my aikido philosophy is to adopt the kaizen approach daily, 'a step at a time'. My attitude is that I will do my best today and see how far I can go and continuously improve on my aikido bit by bit. I am confident that some progress should emerge and be noticed (well, I would like to think so!).

The truth is that by maintaining this kaizen attitude daily not only helps me and my aikido but also has additional benefits beyond my practice. It helps me as an individual to overcome the daily challenges I encounter and sees that I can cope with the daily events and situations related to my work, private life and so on.

Aikido has this amazing ability to help ourselves. Indeed, when we practice aikido techniques on the mats and apply specific principles with circles, triangles, square and spirals, these movements do affect us, our mind and spirit, for the better. Our behavioural attitude changes the way we respond to difficult situations, helping us with a 'stay calm and carry on' spirit, finding a positive outcome that will provide all parties a win-win situation (not always possible, but we will surely try our best to find this ideal solution). Aikido has this ability to subconsciously help us.

That is why I believe, for as long as I live, in continuing practicing aikido, as it has helped me tremendously in building who I am today.

I also believe that aikido has a way to keep us active and stay in tune with our body, mind and spirit. When we get old, we continue to believe we can practice aikido and therefore our mind beats our age limit. We are witnessing so many of our senior instructors who are over 60 or even over 70 still practicing as if age has no limit – aikido helps them maintain their spirit sharp. Some may practice other forms such as yoga or meditation but there is no doubt that aikido has given them the strength and will power to practice such disciplines.

To me, it is clear that they follow the kaizen approach and I cannot help but admire their passion and spirit that continues to thrive and motivates them to learn aikido. From watching our senior instructors, I cannot help but continue with burning desire to practice aikido with kaizen approach...

Could Aikido Be of Help to Mental Health Sufferers?

Early hours this morning I was having my breakfast watching *Good Morning Britain* on TV. Susanna Reid and Alastair Campbell were discussing serious concerns about mental health, as more British people are having a mental health breakdown. It was said that one in four British is now having mental health issues due to Covid-19 and all the restrictions applied together with social distancing. Sadly, it was added that this trend on the increase like a silent and invisible disease.

Mental health used to be very much a taboo and no one would be really talking about it years ago, until recently things changed. It is frightening to know that many men under the age of 45 commit suicide in UK, the highest suicide rate being for men aged 45-49.

There are many factors that make men more vulnerable to suicide. Men are often under pressure to appear strong and not show signs of weakness. This means they are less likely to talk about any issues they are facing or seek help when they are struggling with their mental health.

Sometimes pride comes into the equation and men may think they can handle their issues on their own or maybe they worry about being a burden to others. Men are also more likely to respond to stress with risky behaviour such as abusing alcohol, which increases the risk of suicide by up to eight times.[3]

A relationship breakdown has a bigger impact on a man's suicide risk than a woman's – divorced men are three times more likely to commit suicide than their married peers, whereas divorced women show no increased risk.

[3] https://www.samaritans.org/policy/alcohol-misuse

Thanks to Prince William, Princess Kate and Harry, a bold decision to raise mental health awareness was taken and now the Government is recognising that mental health is to be tackled within the NHS.

On that *Good Morning Britain* program, Doctor Hilary Jones was highlighting for everyone that there is no quick fix to this problem. Due to Covid-19, the NHS is massively struggling with all the patients booking for urgent appointments, operations, after care. There are simply not enough staff to cope with the insurgence of mental health sufferers. We are still in the pandemic crisis.

I deeply reflected on what it had been said. I am not suggesting to have the solution to this crisis, but I was thinking about my personal situation, at how if I had not discovered aikido perhaps I could have been one of these affected mental health patients. I will never know it, to be honest.

One thing I can say, though, is that I have aikido, which helped me over the years to have a sense of purpose in my life, to find my inner strength, to accept when I fail or struggle to succeed or to manage a situation or a number of situations. Somehow aikido helps me to get up every time I fall – just like uke taking a breakfall, you keep standing up from falls.

So one would think that uke is 'losing' the battle but in aikido, this is way deeper than that: uke is not a 'loser', so to speak, but someone who learns to adapt and take on the challenge, to respond as it comes and find strength within it - just like we find our own centre when we take a breakfall, so we are immediately alert and ready for the next challenge.

Wouldn't this be something that some mental health sufferers would want to feel or learn to become strong? In order for them to cope with their feelings in a more positive way? I would hope so.

We are all human beings at the end of the day and everyone will struggle with their challenges daily. So it is crucial to find our 'place' where we know we feel safe and where we can build or even re-build our strength – to me this place is aikido.

We know that in recent years, there has been a decline in interest for martial arts, as young generations appeared to be more focused on technology and prefer studying something that is quick to master - unlike aikido, that would take years and years of practice before seeing any great results. Wouldn't it be great if we could encourage them to take on a new challenge or embrace a new resolution and take on a new martial art? Karate, judo, taekwondo, kung fu, krav maga, kickboxing, boxing, or even aikido?

Not all mental health sufferers may be able to undertake a physical activity but for those who physically would, I believe that in the long run it could bring enormous benefits. They would quickly learn to focus on something during practice and for that hour or two of training they would completely forget their worries. It would offer them positive relaxation, releasing the good enzymes feeling, which is excellent for our physique and well-being. We know that the serum activities of those enzymes, that are found especially in the muscles - particularly creatine kinase - increase in proportion to the intensity and duration of the preceding exercise, peaking 24 hours after exercising.

When you experience an activity where you begin to relax and enjoy, one will want to return and experience more of that, like I do when I practice aikido – any worries or stress I may feel from work is completely forgotten during my two hours of practice. After a session, I actually feel great and more relax than I was before the session.

Some mental health sufferers may be lonely, lacking confidence, feeling depressed or even suffering from a post traumatic experience that left them afraid of failing. It may be very hard for them to try and return to normality without speaking with someone or doing some form of physical activity to unwind their feelings or anxieties.

I think that taking up a martial art like aikido could help them, because not only it provides good physical activity but also because it offers much more than this, with its philosophical approach and with the engaging of our body, mind and spirit.

I can speak about aikido, as I am a practitioner of this Art, but I am certain that anyone practicing any other martial art would share my views on the many additional benefits that a martial art would offer rather than just going to the gym.

If one wishes to learn aikido, for instance, I can name so many benefits that we cannot find in the gym:

- we learn that aikido is a discipline, so we respect one another;
- we learn to train with a good heart, keeping our ego in check and becoming humbler;
- we learn to apply the techniques involving our body, mind and spirit to make them work together;
- we learn to stay calm and to empty our mind when faced with multiple attackers;
- we learn how to increase our sense of awareness;
- we learn to feel one another through touch or human contact;
- we learn to use good body posture, and know where the power

comes from;
- we learn to relax when applying techniques;
- we learn to blend with our partner in a way that we have the upper hand in the situation, and so on.

Personally, I see the above as huge assets in helping mental health sufferers. Aikido is obviously not for everyone but you can see my thinking here. My experience with my own struggles and challenges with my hearing disability has been so positive that I was able to overcome them and even went much further. I went travelling abroad, learned another language and set up a business 17 years ago (still running to date). Now I am employing around 98 members of staff working on our clients sites across London and the South East, providing on-site staffing solutions within the residential and commercial sector.[4] From watching *Good morning Britain* this morning, I felt like writing this chapter to show that there are things that we can do to help our community.

The big question is, "How do we reach out to them and let them know about trying aikido (or martial arts)?". I am convinced that it can be of help to find a focus and a purpose in their life.

Again, I am not saying that taking up a martial art is the answer to resolve all mental health issues. I am merely pointing out that there could be a way, one that has worked for me when I lacked confidence during my teenage time, so it could help some others too.

I think this could be an amazing way to increase our student numbers: to raise awareness that many aikido clubs in the UK (and all other martial arts) would welcome new students and anyone who may be having a difficult time in their life.

Finding a club and meeting new people may be a way to find your new safe place to rebuild your inner strength…

[4] http://www.cledor.co.uk is the company that I set up if you want to check it out.

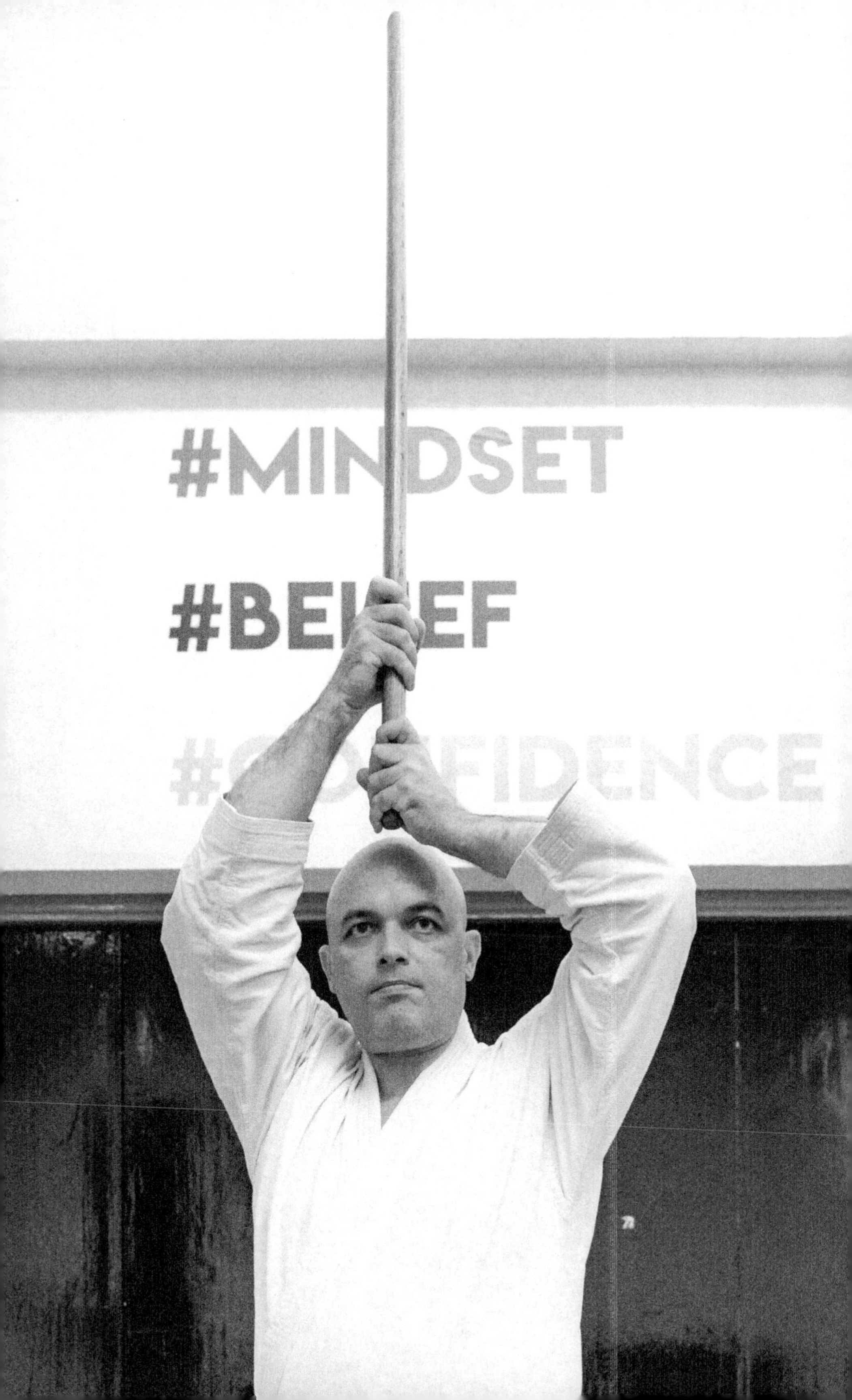
#MINDSET

How Do We Transmit Authentic Aikido to Our Younger Generations?

This question has been on my mind for a considerable amount of time, several years to be fair, and more so lately since I now have been teaching aikido at the Aspire Aikido London Dojo.

In fact, years ago I made a personal promise to myself to do all I can to preserve and teach the authentic aikido that I learnt from all my teachers, as I continue to learn - today and for the years to come - improving my aikido for as long as I may continue, for the rest of my life.

Teaching aikido holds me dear, and my heart tells me very clearly that if aikido is to continue to exist in the form that I know or learnt, I must ensure I transmit all I know wholeheartedly, so it can be seen as 'authentic' as possible.

If it weren't thanks to Morihiro Saito sensei devoting his life teaching aikido and passing on the knowledge through many great senior teachers who in turn for decades have been passing on the knowledge of this Art worldwide, Iwama Aikido would not have continued the way it is today.

Therefore, I would like to thank all our senior teachers worldwide for doing tirelessly what Morihiro Saito sensei has done – like a candlelight, keeping the flame burning and carrying on with the teaching of this beautiful Art.

This is actually the reason why I have been sharing a number of aikido videos on our Aspire Aikido London Facebook Group, so that each one of us can truly see all the hard work that have been done by each of our senior teachers. We really should thank them all for giving this gift to us to carry on, holding this candlelight for our future generations to come.

To anyone reading this essay, I can testify that aikido works and is effective, as long as you do the right thing, that is apply the techniques correctly, with the right timing and correct positioning of your body.

My life experience has been and is quite unique due to the fact that I have a profound hearing disability. Aikido built my confidence in coping with my disability. I learnt Aikikai and Yoshinkan Aikido before taking up Iwama Ryu Aikido back in 1995, and the fact that I worked as bouncer in night clubs, where I had to experience a number of fights and/or had to evict troublemakers from the premises, prompted me to practically use aikido for several years. Quite often I was outnumbered in fighting situations and aikido has helped me deal with one against many scenarios. Thankfully, Iwama Aikido provides the skills needed to deal with multiple attackers.

Learning aikido has had a profound effect on me, and I personally owe to Morihiro Saito sensei and all my teachers who taught me this Art. As a consequence, it is for me a natural decision to do all I can to transmit in turn this beautiful Art as intact as possible. I would like our future generations to benefit from truly learning what I would call Authentic Aikido from Morihiro Saito sensei, following the lineage of O-sensei who was perfecting this Art in his late years in Iwama.

It is very easy and tempting, as a teacher, to want to make modifications or changes to fit what works for you, and to teach only a selection of techniques that one can do well.

To me, this would be an error of judgement, to follow this path by further transforming the Art and deviating away from all those *aiki* principles that Morihiro Saito sensei tirelessly taught us. To be accurate, for 'transforming' I mean adding a different Art to Iwama Aikido and making a blend of the two.

I am not criticising any instructors who choose to follow this path but I merely stating this for me as a person, that it would be a mistake if I were to do this.

The passing on of Authentic Aikido would simply vanish away, which would be sad if it did. I am hopeful that we, teachers choosing to pass this Art as authentic as possible, may become a candlelight for our younger generations, just as our senior teachers are to us!

We should understand that preserving this Art, unselfishly and with humility, is the best gift we can give, in my view. Aikido is not an Art that we personally created but an Art that we learnt from our teachers who in turn dedicated themselves to passing it on authentically.

Nowadays, we know that there are some serious challenges for aikido schools to find new students due to the current pandemic, and some teachers worldwide are doing their best to attract an audience. They want to create something innovative and flashy to get new students to join in.

I can completely relate to this, as I am too starting a new school and I am familiar with the worries that every teacher would have in mind: "Am I going to have any students in my lesson to cover the dojo financial commitments?"

Without a doubt, we are all going through a difficult time, especially when martial arts schools have had to shut down, following government instructions. Some dojo are experiencing financial pressure and losing more students may make it hard to keep the school open. Some teachers have adapted well in connecting with their students, and are continuing with their teaching of aikido via Zoom classes, or through YouTube videos, or Patreons video links.

Some instructors have been luckier than others, as they operate where the teaching of aikido in the dojo remains authorised. We, in the UK, have only been able to do so for the past few months, when we have finally being able to reopen our schools and launch classes. The pandemic still remains, and we are all learning to live with it and adapt as best as we can. We now know that there must be a balance in order to protect our mental well-being. We cannot remain in lockdown for ever: we must find our way back adapting the best we can.

Some instructors have a special gift, amazing skills and a natural ability to attract a younger audience because they know and understand what the younger generations want to see. The truth is that we must find our way to adapt when dealing with the pandemic, but we also need to find new committed students who may be the future generations of teachers responsible for passing on this beautiful Art to newer generations to come.

If we can find our way to adapt and at the same time teach, with humility, the Art as authentic as possible, it would be the best recipe to ensure that our aikido not only survives but thrives so allowing new talented aikidoka to become the next future pillars of aikido.

My final advice would be to trust and follow your heart, not your ego: the former would lead to a greater success for aikido to thrive while maintaining its authenticity to the fullness.

In my view, we owe this to our future generations to come!

What is Aikido?

This is a question that many of us would surely give a different answer to. If you had asked me years ago, I would have given you a direct answer of what I think aikido is. Now, I know that my answer would be very different, as I believe that my understanding of what aikido is has evolved after practicing it for years. So giving an answer to the 'what is aikido' question can be a fairly difficult task.

For instance, if I was to look at a cup I hold in my hand, I could explain what I see in my cup when I observe it. However, if you are looking at me holding the cup, you may see something slightly different, because from the position you are in, the cup may have a writing or design that is not visible from my angle. If you look at my cup from above, you may see the inside of the cup better than I do. So, we could reach different understandings and yet, we are all seeing the 'same cup'.

In my view, the cup is what aikido is. It may offer the same challenge for someone to explain it, because when you practice it, each feels something different that cannot be put in words. Therefore, anyone observing our Art without practicing it may never truly understand what you are feeling.

This would also explains why there are various 'styles' in aikido. The masters who have practiced and learnt aikido from the Founder were influenced by their own view and experience in life that deeply affected them in practicing in a specific manner. Their understanding of what is aikido will differ slightly or more deeply from that of other masters.

For these reasons, it is quite difficult to explain to a beginner what aikido is. Some instructors will simply say: "Come and try, or watch a class to get a glimpse of what this is".

Yes, we can simply say it is a Japanese martial arts, that the practice is done using the opponent's force to subdue him/her. Even this answer, however, is not always something that people would be fully satisfied with. For me, that would be a partial answer (perhaps enough for a novice to get a glimpse of what aikido it is).

Some say that aikido is a Japanese self-defence martial art derived from aiki-jujitsu plus some throws and other techniques derived from *kenjutsu* and *jojutsu*. I would say that I concur with this explanation because we learn to defend ourselves with this Art, however, when we practice for a while, we gradually discover that aikido is actually not defensive at all, but quite the opposite for that matter. We learn that because of our positioning, tori really initiates or puts uke in a very specific situation voluntarily. Tori is pushing uke to attack in a more specific way and is taking charge of the situation; uke is not leading but is under tori's control. In keeping with this principle, aikido is no longer an art of 'self-defense', that is, where you react to an attack. Indeed, tori would initiate or create an opening, which would 'lay the trap ahead' for uke to 'step in'. Then, tori executes possible aikido techniques respecting specific principles such as the shapes of triangle (hanmi with footwork), square (hips/stability/posture), circle (movement/non-static) and spirals up and down or sideways or laterally - all of this while using kokyu (breathing power), understanding *mae* (distance between tori/uke with taijutsu and bukiwaza), applying atemi (strikes) when they are needed to be applied, awase (blending), *meguri* (spinning of hands or hips), zanshin (awareness and stillness at the end of the technique), *kiai* (shout from *hara* releasing energy with our body, mind and spirit at once). Tori can overcome the situation by controlling uke by applying the above principles.

In my opinion, this would be a better explanation of what aikido is than those previously mentioned, but would this explanation be too much for an outsider to hear and understand? I would think so.

As aikidoka, we are always faced with this challenge to explain what is aikido in the simplest way possible. Indeed, the answer has to be kept short but complete enough to keep one's interest alive, or even better to motivate him in trying aikido out by joining a session. A short, clear answer that represents the instructor's point of view and is able to motivate the beginner to discover what aikido is would be perfect.

Recently, I watched a video interview with a very high rank aikido teacher who was asked the same question: "What is aikido?" Interestingly, he gave a whole different explanation as to what aikido is. His answer was very insightful, and it touched me quite a lot, as it related to us as human beings and how we engage and interact with each other, as opposed to explaining what is aikido and how we practice aikido technically on the mats.

To him, aikido has the tools to unite people and bring them together as a family: with this in mind, we preserve peace. He went further saying that aikido connects people's hearts and emotions. He also believes that aikido is indeed very effective but only if one practices honestly with real attacks. He elaborated that it is the only way to understand how and when we should move. This is how we get to learn aikido physical movements while maintaining a good posture, but also using a specific mental attitude of emptiness when dealing with the 'now moment' and working with meguri.

As a result, aikido offers a way to connect people and to preserve mutual peace. He also explains beautifully that when we meet someone who is angry, aikido has a way to create a connection where we isolate the enemy (Anger). We create a balance between uke and tori, where both are not mad at each other but find a way to reconcile and restore peace through the execution of very specific aikido techniques and we get to understand that the enemy is a 'third person'.

He went on to elaborate that when real attacks are executed, and good aikido technique is applied using meguri - we know that spirals are prominent in aikido techniques - they affect our inner being for the better and touch our emotional feelings deeply. This is why aikido helps us to become better human beings, if we practice diligently. One can say that aikido is a manifestation of Love.

I thought his explanation was lovely to hear and beautiful and I could relate with his explanation from where I am with my training. If someone had said this to me years ago, when I was a beginner, I would have thought 'he is a bit mad' to say such things. If you are a novice, actually, you may even agree with this thought.

Some go so far as to say that aikido has the tools to promote spiritual enlightenment, as it helps people feel happy and share this wonderful spiritual experience with others.

If you have read so far, you may agree that it is fair to say that aikido really has many layers with lots of possible explanations that anyone could give other than what I wrote.

The interesting thing is that whenever anyone is asking you what aikido is, at any point of your aikido journey, I am convinced that you may give a different answer.

This also means that aikido is evolving in you at a technical and spiritual level, or that you are evolving with aikido!

To me, this explains why aikido is a very advanced martial arts and profound in many ways, both technically and spiritually.

Overall, to explain as accurately as possible what aikido is, I would finally say that it is essential to practice this Art with a good heart and true honesty, and to work on improving your techniques constantly so that they remain effective. This would be the right way to practice a good aikido and to explain what aikido is...

Is Aikido Effective?

Well, of course you would be expecting my answer to be "yes, aikido is effective!", as I am an aikido practitioner and I love this martial art, so naturally I would advocate it.

However, to be truly honest, each aikidoka should ask this question to themselves every now and then, when studying aikido.

I can only speak for myself and I will say this: "Each time I practice or teach, I strive to practice an aikido that works with effective aikido techniques". I understand that we are all individuals, as Tony Sargeant sensei wisely said in his recent successful aikido seminar back in September 2021. Inevitably, some aikidoka will have a penchant to practice aikido more spiritually than martially, or they will use aikido as a way 'to communicate' with their body and feelings, and they will be less focused or worried about the martial aspects that aikido offers.

I do respect any different approach, however, it is not a path I have or would personally consider, and I genuinely do not mean to criticise anyone. The way I see aikido from my perspective is that each one of us has to climb a mountain, which seems impossible at first. Each of us must find our own individual path to reach a higher level, one step at a time, reflect and carry on with the 'climbing'.

We can all agree that there are multiple paths that we are all free to choose from, but we must accept that some paths will lead towards the top, whereas some will simply lead to an impasse.

This would naturally lead to another question: "How would I know if my aikido works?".I can only offer my answer based on my experience to date of aikido training in the dojo and outside of it.

Some may already know about my past work experience working as a 'bouncer' in night clubs. It would be fair to say that I had my good share of real fighting situations which quickly helped me understand some very crucial elements that make our aikido effective and/or ineffective.

I also would like to reassure anyone that you do not have to go through what I have experienced with real fights to understand or to test your aikido! It was indeed a risky experience that I would not advocate that you follow. Based on my experience, here are the main points that I am happy to share in order to help you understand if your aikido is effective or not.

I am going to focus on what makes aikido effective rather than the opposite. In my view, we must first of all control our partner's balance. He may be the quickest fighter, but if his balance is broken, he will not be able to fight back.

Our brain is simply conditioned 'to be feeling grounded on our feet or balanced' before we can retaliate. It is a fact in regard to who we are and how we function as human beings. It is very important to remember that!

If you understand this, you will inevitably work on doing an aikido that affects your partner's balance from start to finish and in my view you will be on a solid path to build a strong and effective aikido.

This is not enough, however, there are still a few more points that one should need bearing in mind.

The next essential thing is to make sure that when performing a technique you use your body properly, to be exact your hips must move and be connected with the technique. Fact: your hips are the biggest joints of your body, so the effect will be far more powerful than the joints of your shoulders, which are smaller than the hips.

As a consequence, if you work with your hips you can overcome someone taller and stronger! Use your hips instead of your upper body, which will help you build a stronger and more effective aikido.

I would then add the next important point asking a question: "Are you in the best position to handle multiple attackers at any points? Is your body positioned correctly at the right time and location?"

If your aikido is just working on 'one to one' basis, then it will have its limitations with 'one to one' only, so if you are faced with multiple attackers, you could potentially put yourself at risk. I learnt this from real fighting situations.

To remedy this, adopt a different mindset: feel that you are surrounded all the time. Indeed, if you focus on the one against multiple attackers situation rather than on the one on one with your partner, you will be surprised how easily you will overcome your partner. Why is that? Because your mind is no longer just focusing on your partner, but you are now extending your awareness toward what may come next. I invite you to try this and you may find that your aikido will be on another level of consciousness.

It is also fair to say that aikido effectiveness seats on a 'thread', so to speak, meaning that it can easily become useless, if we are not moving at the right time and location. This naturally brings awase into the equation, an important element in keeping our aikido effective.

Interestingly, the word awase is not mentioned frequently within the Aikikai, while is prominently quoted in Iwama Aikido due to its extensive bukiwaza training. Again, it is an observation and not a criticism.

Finding perfect awase is not easy: if we move too early, the attacker can deviate or change the attack; if we move too late, the attacker will successfully attack us as we would be too late to respond.

Perfect awase to me is not just 'moving as one' with your partner but moving when the he has reached the point where his attack can no longer be changed or redirected, in another words, the attack is fully committed.

Keeping the above in mind, awase is possibly the hardest thing to do, hence why it takes years of bukiwaza practice, which helps our taijutsu tremendously. To make this possible, one must adopt an empty mind and live in the 'now' moment. Also hard to do…

Truly speaking, you can see that to make aikido effective, one must work on its physical aspect but also use your mind to focus properly and connect with the partner as 'one' unity moving together.

When we work with awase, we experience a deep feeling of being between 'life' and 'death'. In its true terms, one lives (tori) and one dies (uke), just like when we do ken practice in a *kumitachi*.

If we pick irimi nage, for instance, it is a technique that requires tori to step in behind uke's attack or behind uke's body. The 'stepping behind uke' is a difficult one to accomplish, as it must be done with the correct timing (awase) and there must be a feeling of 'it was close', meaning a second too late, I would not have made it, a second earlier it would have been too early.

Another important point is to keep atemi where they are meant to be! I understand that some people dislike atemi, because perhaps they think they do not have a place in 'spiritual' aikido. If one thinks atemi are not necessary, in my view is going toward an impasse.

Atemi are there for a reason, to preoccupy uke's mind, for him to block with the other hand whilst you move for the next step, affecting his balance further.

Truly speaking, we are frequently practicing 'on a thread' between what I would call effective and useless aikido. To stay on this narrow path or 'thread', one must and should question frequently if our aikido is still effective or not. This is if you wish it to retain its full martial benefits.

Some say that aikido techniques don't work. I firmly disagree with this approach. Techniques, if properly executed, are designed to work. If you are struggling to make the technique work, it would be because you are not applying the technique correctly. Some techniques will take years of repeated practice before understanding how to apply them.

It is very easy to lose the martial aspect in aikido and create something that looks great but would never work outside the dojo. Sometimes we see this when one always trains with the same partners. Hence why I think we must train with different people all the time: training with the same partner over a period of time could cause another well-known issue: uke could very easily cooperate or offer no resistance when he actually could. Also, very often uke knows what is happening so he is no longer training in the moment (now), so to speak, but is already thinking of the ending before it has happened! This means that tori can easily fall into thinking that his aikido is good or working when it isn't.

In conclusion, I think the key is to be honest with ourselves and speak from the heart, not from our ego. The truth may be unpleasant for anyone, but I am certain that it will take you to a whole new level of learning: like a new path reaching a higher level, with each one of us climbing the mountain which is aikido…

Good Body Posture Brings Power

It recently occurred to me that if we had not gone into national lockdown due to pandemic situation with Covid-19, I would not have felt what I now feel to be so prominent and strong when I practice aikido focusing on my own body posture.

Let me elaborate on what I mean by saying this.

Before we entered this global crisis with Covid-19, we aikidoka were all practicing aikido in our dojo or club with a partner or a number of partners, performing lots of aikido techniques unarmed and with weapons, depending on the aikido style you practice.

Speaking for myself as I have been practicing Iwama Aikido and we study a fair amount of weapons and taijutsu with an emphasis on training with one or more partners.

When the national lockdown was announced due to the Covid-19 pandemic, we had to cease any sports activities and martial arts training overnight, so to speak. For many of us, this was extremely hard physically and mentally as well.

At that point, I had a choice of practicing alone or doing nothing and wait until we resumed our normal practice, hoping for the best that the pandemic would stop. As you know, however, it went on (and it still is) for nearly 18 months in the UK, during which we were heavily restricted to resume with our normal practice in with other people.

Therefore if I had made a decision to pause any aikido training until we could resume, it would have meant 18 months of no training (sadly, I know some aikidoka who did just that). I am very glad that I did not choose this option!

I began practicing on my own in my garden and I was very determined to do this for as long as it would take.

I also recorded my practice and shared the videos on my YouTube channel, which turned out to be an exciting project (which kept me busy while killing time in isolation). I also realised that by doing this, I could help and encourage others to do the same and carry on with their own solo practice. I know a few aikidoka who have done just that and were inspired by the frequent video releases on my YouTube Channel.

It is fair to say, that this decision was probably the best I have ever taken for myself and my aikido, as I learnt tremendously without having a 'Teacher' - although, to be more accurate, there was a 'Teacher', who was 'me' analysing any videos I made. This process made me very critical in correcting myself and it brought huge benefits, as I felt I was self-learning and improving my aikido.

This project not only helped my aikido but it also helped me cope with my mental health. It made me stay positive despite isolation and strong when things did look pretty grim after learning about the devastating effects that Covid-19 had on so many people in the UK and the rest of the world...

My solo training helped me to focus but also made me realise the meaning of an important sentence that I had heard many times before but had never sufficiently 'sunk' into my body: "Good posture brings good power".

Let me explain. We may have heard this statement before from our teacher when practicing with a partner, but many of us still neglected it and compromised our posture to subdue our partner, as we believe this is what aikido is about, isn't it? Our posture can become 'slightly compromised' but we think it is still OK as long as we can pin down or throw our partner...

To be frank, the national lockdown got me to do solo training and got me to understand and appreciate this sentence better and to apply it more consciously than ever before, since we were not allowed to practice with anyone outside our home and no contact was possible.

Many martial artists and notably aikidoka in many parts of the world, especially where weapons practice is not taught a lot, were quite limited in continuing to practice aikido. As I practice Iwama Aikido, I quickly realised how lucky we were to have all the wonderful bukiwaza syllabus that Morihiro Saito sensei has left us. We could do it all outside, in a park or garden, and it felt even more wonderful than practicing them in the dojo, as we could sense a deeper connection with nature around us.

Iwama Aikido bukiwaza includes the following: 7 Ken Suburi, 20 Jo Suburi, 13 Jo Kata (solo & paired practice), 31 Jo Kata (solo & paired practice), 7 Kumitachi (and Henka), Ki Misubi No Tachi, 10 Kumijo (and Henka), 10 old Ken Tai Jo, 7 new Ken Tai Jo (and Henka), 18 Lost Jo Kata, 20 Jo Fluid Form, 7 Ken Suburi No Kata etc.

You can see by just mentioning all these that we were (and are) benefiting from a huge amount of weapons techniques that one can practice alone. This even includes all the paired practice that one can do alone imagining a partner attacking you in a specific way. It is possible to perform a kumitachi from tori side or from the uke side and create awase in your mind.

This is exactly what I did for the entire duration of the lockdown. I kept practicing alone, working on the bukiwaza syllabus and I gradually benefited from doing it – at times I self corrected myself and worked on improving my technique in terms of posture, feet placement, hips and timing, etc.

If you are interested, you can see all these videos that are freely accessible on my YouTube channel in a specific playlist.[5]

The solo practice I have been doing gave me deeper feeling and understanding on how important it is to have a good posture. Hence why I advocate this: 'good posture brings power'.

Now that I am back teaching and practicing aikido, I see this even more clearly than ever before. We should not focus on trying to subdue our partner but on our own body posture. Finding the correct hips positioning with correct footwork is my primary goal, which will naturally affect my partner's posture (and without trying hard too).

I am convinced that good posture brings a more powerful aikido, without having to try tensing our muscles, and feeling from our hips or hara instead (the inner feeling). Studying weapons (aikiken and aikijo) will help you find very specific body shapes such as *hitoemi,* for instance.

I think if one does not practice weapons, they may not fully 'feel' what the hitoemi positioning means, which is developed thanks to the practice of the 2nd Ken Suburi.

Please note that I am only referring about Iwama Aikido so this is not intended to criticise other aikido styles as each aikido style offers

[5] https://www.youtube.com/c/nickregnier1

something truly unique!

So, if one aikidoka is not practicing weapons enough, they may not experience (inside) the feeling of hitoemi, although they may be able to do the physical form of a hitoemi stance. It may still be 'empty' inside.

That is why my constant solo training during the pandemic helped me develop further my inner feeling.

I also come to realise that the study of weapons is not really to merely use the weapons per se, but to teach our body the correct feet movement and placement, to feel our hips moving in very specific ways, and foremost to experience an inner feeling within the form.

By practicing weapons on your own you practice the inner feeling relative to every form you do, and this is also reflected in your taijutsu practice. In another words, when you practice weapons correctly, you are also practicing your taijutsu (and vice versa!).

If we pick *morote dori kokyu-ho*, this two-hand grip technique is a very specific exercise for building your kokyu feeling and finding hips stability and strength. They can only be felt if the placement of your feet and upper body posture is correct, and the same applies to this inner feeling I referred to when we do bukiwaza.

During the lockdown, I was still able to practice taijutsu alone in the kihon form, imagining someone firmly gripping my arm. Since no one was grabbing me, there was a strange sensation building from my own centre. I could feel the kokyu building in my arms and forming a united feeling with the centre from hips and feet positioning. I immediately felt it work on my own posture to make sure my back was straight, that I was moving as one with hips, hand and feet.

The entire solo practice I was doing became an absolute joy to experience and I discovered another side of aikido training that I would never have felt before, that is doing aikido without a partner.

The inner sensation grew even stronger and when we resumed our normal practice again, when I practice morote dori kokyu-ho I now do it differently: my focus is to retain a good posture and by achieving this, I noticed that my partner was more affected, as there was no longer thinking of dropping him to the ground. The better the posture you adopt, the more your partner's posture is naturally affected. Together with kokyu, a number of other principles as to be followed: precise hanmi, keeping your elbows low, connecting with the partner and getting close enough, etc.

So, I would strongly encourage anyone to analyse how you have been practicing your aikido: do you focus on your posture or do you focus on subduing your partner first? I leave this for you to decide...

Benefits with Bowing

One of the elements that made me choose aikido is the fact that there is a strong dojo etiquette where respect is king. In the dojo we see the instructor and students bowing before and at the end of each practice to a photo of O-sensei displayed in the shomen. The students bow to the instructor and bowing also takes place between students before practicing any techniques.

The sign of respect that bowing represents in aikido (and all martial arts) is something that attracted me to learn this Art. Bowing when entering and leaving the dojo has got nothing to do with worshipping: it is ONLY to show our respect.

Some say that bowing is only 'just' like a handshake and that there is nothing more to it. However, if we want to talk about the handshake, I am sure you will agree that you would not be too happy if someone shakes your hand with a dead fish (no shake, no squeeze, no energy) and with poor or no eye contact. You would rather have a good, proper handshake with good eye contact when you meet someone. When it comes to bowing, you will concur that it should not be any different: one should do this properly too.

When we bow, we really use our whole body to make the gesture. We actually sacrifice our body, whereas in a handshake just one limb is involved. I think it is fair to say that the benefits of bowing will be greater than just shaking hands, and I can explain why.

With bowing, we perceive this body gesture from the partner toward us and vice versa, so there is an element of awase in which we want to connect with our partner even if there is no physical contact like a handshake.

When you become accustomed with bowing from training aikido for a while, you will sense the need to perform bowing with humility, showing your honesty and respect towards your partner. A good bowing must be performed without ego and it should be a clean movement done with the right timing and space: you are taking the time to do it properly within a safe distance, rather than doing it quickly and too close, without any meaning or feeling.

To be frank, I should stress that before we can respect anyone else, we, as individual must begin to respect ourselves first. We are doing this by following good hygiene and having a good etiquette. We put a clean *gi*, belt on properly tied up and *hakama* neatly put together, if you are an advanced aikidoka.

When we put on our gi, belt and hakama, it gives us a moment to reflect on how we put our attire together. If I speak for myself, it does give me a moment of reflection and meditation, to get ready for training or for teaching any class.

When we line up at the start of any class, we also wait for our instructor to be at the front of the class and we all bow to O-sensei's photo on the *shomen* as a sign of respect. After, we bow to our instructor teaching the class and we say "*Onegaishimasu*", which has quite a few meanings but I believe we say it with the meaning "please teach us". We also say this with gratitude, generosity, resilience, open mind and cooperation in mind.

During practice, the bowing with our partners is done simultaneously and if you do it correctly, that is with humility, you will feel a sense of purification in your mind and heart and you will develop a positive feeling when you practice aikido with your partner(s).

At the end of every session, we bow to our teacher and our partners we trained with by saying "*Domo Arigato Gozaimashita*", "Thank you very much" in Japanese.

If we bow the wrong way, without humility, soon we will experience serious limitations in learning the Art deeper. I have said before that aikido techniques are only 'revealed' when we have the right mindset (and skills too). Those who would want to learn aikido for ill intent or evil purposes will not be able to progress very far. The instructor would ask them to leave the dojo immediately. The instructor covers an important role to play: he is there not only to teach but to ensure that the students can safely practice aikido without fear of any injuries.

In my experience, I have seen how gracious and beautiful aikido techniques can be when a senior instructor has attained many years of aikido experience and their bowing is different than the beginners' bowing. Their aikido contains something special as they get older (and wiser) that many young practitioners cannot attain or copy, because their understanding of aikido is not on the same level as them.

It would be quite normal to think that a senior instructor would be on another level of aikido understanding than the younger generations, just as they were when they were young, their level of understanding with aikido was different then. We can appreciate their techniques to be 'flowing' effortlessly and becoming 'alive'.

If we watch O-sensei's videos, we can see how clean his movements were and his techniques looked easy to do but I can assure you that they aren't and many of them look rather impossible to achieve still for many of us. O-sensei's aikido was beautiful to watch and we could see how humble he was when he performed precise bowing.

I am convinced that when we train in aikido, we should not neglect our bowing but instead spend some time to practice how to do a good bowing, just the same we do in relation to aikido techniques. One good way to do this is to practice it at home in front of mirror.

Unfortunately, we do see, every now and then, a few aikidoka who fail to bow correctly or that they do a 'semi' or quick bowing, to quickly get to practice techniques with their partner. When you bow, you should do so with your feet together, your hips bringing the upper body forward and down, while keeping your back straight. Your neck should not bend, your eyes should look towards your partner and your hands be placed to the sides of your body side-line, arms down straight, and you should be within a safe distance, so you are not too close or too far from your partner.

To me, bowing correctly means you do this in awase with your partner, but also with zanshin before and during the bowing. Although during the bowing I am sacrificing my body with humility, I retain my zanshin: my partner will sense that I am aware and will not dare to attack during the bowing movement. Sadly, many do not apply zanshin when bowing and 'trust' their partner too much or too easily.

Finally, when you perform good bowing, your aikido will begin to affect you as a person simply because you will be more open and connected with your heart, which will gradually change your aikido with extra sensitivity through zanshin.

After explaining what constitute a good bowing, an experienced aikidoka can see another person's level of aikido by watching how they perform their bowing, just like from the way they tie their belts.

My final advice would be to 'connect' with your heart and seek humility during practice but also when bowing...

#MINDSET
#BELIEF

Why Being a Good 'Uke' is Better Than Being a Good 'Tori'

Quite a few aikidoka have not even thought about this question deeply. Many believe that we 'learn' aikido when we are tori by executing techniques and so they need 'someone', an uke, to train with in order to learn aikido. With that in mind, they also think that uke is 'sacrificing' his time receiving and waiting for their turn to be tori again.

If you think this is the case, then I would ask you to take a moment to read my post further, as I am convinced you are only learning a fraction of what aikido is...

The tori-uke relationship is very much like *yin* and *yang*, each being the opposite of other, but truly needing each other to form a complete shape and therefore each side is equally important. There is no difference between tori and uke, apart from the fact that when you learn to be a good uke, you will understand the technique better. This is why I say that being a good uke is more important than being a good tori. Why is that?

Well, I can explain again from my experience in practicing this Art for the past 32 years. I can relate several reasons that led me to understand why being a good uke is really crucial to understanding aikido, to truly know how the techniques work and simply realise when they don't.

During practice, too often I notice aikidoka who simply disregard their attention to being a good uke, like how to perform a good breakfall. Some aikidoka are better at being tori than at being uke, so to speak. This is partially because they believe aikido is when tori performs techniques, so they don't pay much attention on how to maintain their composure when they lose their balance.

Frequently, some aikidoka will 'quickly' fall down when tori performs a pinning technique such as *ikkyo, nikkyo, sankyo, yonkyo* or *gokyo*. They

71

drop down quite easily losing their composure or more precisely, losing their 'centre'. I could say the same thing when they get up after a pinning technique is finished.

I tried to understand why I see this with quite a few aikidoka and I guess they respond in this manner to avoid any potential pain a pinning technique could inflict, so they give themselves up quickly waiting for their turn as tori to execute the same technique...

Some of you may say that it would be the instructor's fault for not teaching breakfalls enough to their students. I would concur if there is little of this taught in classes.

To me, falling is an important part for any aikidoka. Uke should retain their composure when they lose their balance, also they should retain their centre during any fall and likewise when they get up on their feet.

Also, uke needs to feel the pinning technique to understand it, that way they will develop extra sensitivity and be cautious when applying this technique on their partner.

I notice a lack of zanshin. Indeed quite a few uke tend to 'switch off' their zanshin as soon as they lose their balance and when they get up as well. Their zanshin is back again when get ready to attack, like a switch going on and off frequently.

When you step on the mat, your zanshin should be on permanently, during the whole session, so the 'switching on-off' should have no place during any session.

To me, being a good uke means to find a way to keep my centre (and zanshin) even when I fall in any direction!

Another benefit from this correct attitude is that uke learns to build sensitivity with tori. If tori throws you gently, you should feel their intention and adapt your fall to be gentle manner, by keeping your centre and zanshin; if tori throws you harder, you would feel the intention and swiftly adapt, hence doing a high breakfall instead of a normal rolling one.

By the way, this is also worth mentioning: if tori is applying a technique on uke fast, it would be right to assume that uke has got enough experience to manage such situation and that he can fall safely and well. Tori should not do this if uke is not ready to take advanced breakfalls.

Learning to fall as an uke truly teaches you to understand how the technique works, or when it begins to work. Consequently, when you are tori, you will know how to subdue your uke more effectively using a certain position or angle that affect his balance.

Another common issue is when uke stiffens excessively during a fall or pin, which could have the potential to hurt them more than if they had remained relaxed. Being a good uke means you should stay relaxed and centred, thus you will be in a better position to handle the technique.

I guess the tension comes into play when uke is anxious about certain techniques that tori may be doing. This would be for several reasons: uke may have had a bad injury and is fearing a repeat of the same or another injury; or uke could be apprehensive as he is not so confident in doing a forward or backward breakfall, for instance.

One way to tackle this kind of fear in uke, is for tori to guide uke in a way not to hurt their partner, only going as far as uke can go with confidence. Bit by bit, tori can repeat the technique by adding more to it when uke, over time, is more ready.

If uke is more experienced than tori, it would be quite easy for uke to make it more difficult for tori to perform a technique properly, as uke would know how to block or prevent their partner from executing a particular technique. Uke should avoid this and allow a less experienced tori to do the technique and guide their partner, fostering a good mutual practice. Otherwise, it would be quite frustrating for tori to be constantly blocked.

However, if tori is more experienced than uke, then I feel that uke should be a little bit more honest with tori, meaning to remain strong where possible. This would give a better chance for tori to know if his technique is correctly done or where they need to practice more to improve their aikido.

Bearing in mind the above, we should avoid any wrestling or any ill feeling to prove a point to our partner. It would mean we are being guided by our ego and not by our heart. It is very important to always train with a good heart and to offer our time to assist our partner in the best way possible. Both tori and uke can truly benefit a very good session by bearing this in mind at all time.

When you practice your breakfalls (forward, backward and sideways), keep your zanshin at all times, understand when you are beginning to lose your balance, know how you keep your composure using your centre and, maintaining kokyu feeling in your hands.

When all these are in place, I can confidently say that you will begin to discover how and when techniques work, so when you are tori you will achieve a deeper understanding of the techniques and an increased sensitivity.

Being a good uke will make you a stronger tori!

Steven
Seagal

ABOVE
THE
LAW

Has Aikido Lost its Touch?

To be frank, quite a few of you reading this title may simply say that I just gave this away by saying it. Many will also agree that aikido has 'lost' its touch since its prime time, in the 80s and 90s, when it was extremely popular and millions of people around the world joined martial arts.

In this era, learning martial arts became a rapid phenomenon thanks to the emergence of Bruce Lee's films and notably Steven Seagal, who did an excellent job in promoting aikido in the 90s with the famous *Nico* movie - and other films he did after this one.

Many now dislike Steven Seagal for who he has become, but we cannot deny the fact that he has really promoted aikido worldwide thanks to his films and that many simply joined this martial art after watching him in action.

I remember being 15 years of age when I watched his film for the first time and without knowing what it was about, and I was shocked that this guy could beat people real bad even when outnumbered. Soon after watching *Nico*, I had to check what martial arts he was doing and I was instantly 'sold' to doing aikido.

Many would even say: "Who cares if aikido lost its touch? When O-sensei was teaching aikido he had very few students compared to what we now have worldwide and if it makes you happy then that is all you need to be worried about." I respect this opinion, still I would not be satisfied as to why aikido would have 'lost its touch'. I still think that we need to understand why many believe in the title of this chapter to be true, if we love aikido this much (like I do)!

I have been practicing aikido for over 32 years and I have trained with various instructors and learnt different styles of aikido before Iwama

Aikido. I have seen what works and what does not in my years of bouncer work in night clubs, so I can see why aikido has lost its touch to a degree. Please allow me to explain.

Firstly, I want to appease anyone's mind that this is not a point stating that Iwama Aikido is the strongest and the best of all the styles. I believe that any good instructor teaching any style of aikido can build strong students for the future generations and for them to possibly take the lead by becoming new teachers.

If you have read the chapter *Introduction to Aikido* that opens this book, you will know that I was at a cross point with aikido and nearly gave it up when I found a book of Morihiro Saito sensei. In that book he stated that if you want to learn strong aikido, you should learn bukiwaza and so I did. That experience helped me to be who I am today and to continue practicing and now teaching aikido. As a matter of fact, anyone's experience will certainly differ from mine and I also wish to reassure that some could find the right instructor within the Aikikai, Birankai, Yoshinkan, or Ki Society Aikido, just to name a few.

My main issue, if we stick to the subject of this essay, is that there are lots of aikido teachers who teach aikido techniques that will never work outside of the dojo. Some may even be aware of this and don't really care, as the sharing that type of Art is giving them a great feeling. The students happily comply and go with the flow to create beautiful fancy movements that look elegant and almost as if uke is no longer attacking. If that is what they wish to do and they get students happy to do this kind of training, then, who am I to say criticise them? I would say great for them wholeheartedly and I wish them my best for what they want to do.

However, here I am referring to what members of the public, as far as they are concerned, would truly think of aikido when they see such 'compliance', and to those who practice another martial art: they would immediately notice that something isn't right with this extreme compliance full of 'openings' (weak angles) in their movements.

Again, this group of aikidoka can quite rightly say: "Who cares? We are happy doing what we are doing". Who am I to judge them? And they would be right to put me in my place, so to speak. What I can say is that they are judged by 'external people' (who do not practice aikido) who will give aikido a negative reputation. This negative reputation can be damaging for the community that teaches good aikido as far as I am concerned, if I can speak bluntly.

Another issue that I see is that in some styles aikido has changed quite a lot from previous generations to the present. If we see the Doshu and his son Dojo-Cho Mitsuteru Ueshiba, we can see that there is very strong aikido lineage and that it is passed on faithfully from father to son and that the Aikikai Hombu Dojo does have a strong future ahead.

However, there are some groups of aikido where divergence can be noticed from one generation to the next, and that there is too much of a change. As a result of this, aikido has now lost its effectiveness.

Some say aikido evolves. I would concur but we need to make sure it evolves keeping all the right principles in place or we simply deviate away from what O-sensei taught. Some people would probably love to ask me: What are the principles of aikido? This would lead to a whole new topic, but I am sure that many would concur with what I have been writing so far.

Some may say that O-sensei made lots of changes and created his own martial art now known as aikido, implying that we are 'free' to do the same and that "Aikido needs to evolve". Frankly speaking, however, I have not seen anyone to date as talented as O-sensei. I think it would be quite pretentious for anyone to claim that they have reached O-sensei's level of skills in martial arts to justify embarking on modifications or alterations or creating something completely new or unprecedented.

The truth is that no one got even near to what O-sensei was in terms of martial skills to this day – and why is that?

Well, we live in a different society and one cannot possibly train hours of martial arts daily, as many of us have to work to feed our families. We simply do not have the time that O-sensei had in his lifetime.

For me, this all leads to the realisation that aikido is not mine, but it is for me to share what it is for others to understand it. It is a vast subject, to be fair, and this would lead to another discussion about preserving the Art as best as possible. I wrote an essay specifically about this topic, *How do we transmit authentic aikido to our younger generations* - kindly refer to it.

In my view, aikido "has lost its touch" WHEN teachers teach things that will not work in reality. Some say that there are too many clubs, too many instructors given ranks that yet do not have the skills to teach the Art correctly. Therefore, it would be best that aikido 'shrinks' with fewer teachers and for those who remain to be those who have been successful in teaching strong and good aikido that meets the needs of new generations. To keep 'aikido in touch', we should understand what young generations are looking for to or expecting to see. I have noticed that aikido, which used to be enjoyed by the younger generations of the past, now become older generations but still training faithfully, while we see a decline in membership among the younger new generations.

Could it be that the young generations have it all too easy? Meaning that parents will provide for their kids with all the technology they want, mobile phone, tablets, PC, computer games, etc, that they no longer want to work hard to get it? Many prefer to do MMA, or BJJ or other new boxing arts, because they are quick to learn. You will get to a certain level fast and once you get there, most will tend to stop and cease to attend.

As you know, aikido really takes years of practice to get to a good level and when someone gets serious about it, they will soon realise that it will be a lifetime journey of great enjoyment and discovery, where one never stops learning and progressing until we can no longer practice or until we pass.

Does this mean that this it is 'too much to take in' for our younger generations? I don't really know the answer, to be fair. However, I have had numerous discussions with several teachers and I discovered that the ones who have been successful in teaching aikido and in attracting the younger generations are simply answering to their needs:
- They want to see something dynamic, so the teacher will show dynamic aikido;
- They want to see real punches and what one can do to defend themselves so they show this side of aikido;
- Some want to see kicks, so again they show this side and once they see that yes aikido works,
- They want to see if it works against multiple attackers, so they get to see this from the teacher.

Quite cleverly, the teacher will gradually show the basic forms so that aikido is taught keeping all the principles in place but with a mixed of dynamic aikido that the public want to see.

Whereas some teachers simply teach the same old aikido that they have been taught years ago, which was OK then but is no longer relevant for the younger generations. I think that we, as teachers, should reflect, step back and see what we can do to make our training more appealing.

I am not proposing to change aikido at all, but to show what aikido can do with all the appealing aspects it offers. I have witnessed some very successful instructors who do just this and things have been working tremendously for them even during pandemic crisis. Bearing this in mind, I would concur that aikido is evolving but it has to do so while keeping all its principles in place to create strong aikido. We must learn to adapt as our society is evolving too.

You see, aikido follows the same principles of the universe, constantly moving our surrounding planets, with Earth travelling at 220 Km per second and revolving around the Sun. The solar system is continuously moving while retaining all its strict rules applied through many principles such as gravity and spirals. Aikido should be doing the same.

Aspire Aikido London's Goal

Aspire Aikido London Dojo is dedicated and committed to follow the teachings of Morihiro Saito sensei that he left us with Takemusu Iwama Aikido, which includes the study of aikiken, aikijo and taijutsu.

Therefore my goal is clear: it is my sheer determination to continue learning the teachings of Takemusu Aikido, and also to further my research in wanting to progress further respecting all the Aiki principles that Morihiro Saito sensei has learnt from the Founder.

For instance, focusing on the body shapes or correct body movement with good stability and hips power is paramount to get it right rather than upper body tensing, which would limit and prevent unleashing true power when techniques are linked with a partner (or multiple partners) executing any forms of attacks.

The correct positioning of feet with hanmi and hips will not only provide the ability to harmonise with uke but also make tori be out of reach of any attacks. I recognise that the latter requires strong awase to be mastered, which is why we will continue studying bukiwaza.

Bukiwaza can help us understand how to blend in and match our partner's speed at any moment and how to achieve fluidity in our movements.

I am truly aware that first, our fundamental basics must be thoroughly practiced, memorising each movement with study of ken and jo. This requires time and continuous efforts for each aikidoka to keep doing.

It is also my clear intention to carry on training with a positive spirit and humility and to work on my individual practice, trying to improve with fresh beginner's eyes. When one has been practicing for years and years, it is always tempting to say: "I know this technique". However, to tell the truth, when adopting the beginner's thinking of "I am here to learn", with this mindset I can feel I am progressing much further.

My determination is to try to further improve my aikido so that I can help my students and all those who wish to learn this beautiful Art.

I am also aware of recent findings that show that when you learn to achieve the right skills and mindset, you begin to see the real secrets that aikido brings, thanks to the study of aikiken and aikijo.

It has become very obvious to me that the study of weapons is not just to learn how to use them as such (although then we do that as well), but to really see how the movement of our body works and especially how everything is set up to deal with the scenario of one against multiple attackers, as also in taijutsu.

This is the reason why aikiken and aikijo cannot be taught separately and are embedded with taijutsu and vice versa, which forms the spirits of Takemusu Aikido. In another words, everything that is taught within aikiken, aikijo and taijutsu has a direct reciprocal link and is extremely logical.

When an aikidoka reaches a high level will understand what Takemusu means! The ability to create an unlimited level of techniques that will suddenly emerge in any given situations, the body leading the way and not the brain...

In one of his published books, Morihiro Saito sensei said that when one attains this Takemusu level, it is a wonderful feeling that he wishes everyone to feel and understand.

I am hoping Aspire Aikido London can do this in time with its existing and future students...

In the meantime, stay safe and well.

Weapons or No Weapons in Aikido?

I understand that this topic has been discussed at length and with huge debates. Many explained their point of view and were persuasive in arguing why to train with weapons or not when practicing aikido. Therefore you could be quite rightly asking, "Why are you writing what could be a 'déja-vu' article?"

Well, I wish to reassure anyone reading this that firstly it is not my intention to divide but to give my honest view, which you are, of course, entitled to agree or disagree with.

Fundamentally, I recognise that it is inevitable that we have our differences of opinion and that this topic has been long debated for many good reasons. It is quite a complex subject, but I think I can keep this discussion relatively simple.

Each one of us is unique, meaning no one will be able to be exactly like O-sensei and vice versa. It is important to recognise that we are all individuals and so our aikido experience will be unique, even if we practice the same aikido representing a specific school. As in painting, there is only one Mona Lisa, so why try to make another? It would be impossible to accomplish.

The interesting thing is that many of our senior instructors who were fortunate to practice under O-sensei all have a different perspective of what aikido is. If we compare Koichi Tohei shihan and Morihiro Saito sensei, we can see that they were very different but yet, they were practicing the same aikido from Founder.

The difference lies with the time and location where they studied the Art under Founder. Morihiro Saito sensei was fortunate to practice with O-sensei for over 23 years in Iwama and often benefited from private tuition with the Founder who was still perfecting his Art: it was in Iwama that the study of aikiken and aikijo began. And yet, Morihiro Saito sensei used to say openly that O-sensei thought Koichi Tohei shihan was his best student of all times.

Throughout O-sensei's lifetime, everyone studying aikido would agree that the Founder was continuously perfecting his aikido, so new techniques were constantly added. Over a period of time, O-sensei made various changes; some techniques had to be altered due to uke finding a way to stop tori from doing the technique itself - for instance, in *katate dori shiho nage*, the starting point used to be with the hara applying a strong pin upward to lift uke, until someone strong enough was able to prevent the lifting, and the technique was then modified. Lots of taijutsu techniques and the weapons study were developed in Iwama after WWII. Aikido was (and still is) new, so it was understandable that O-sensei throughout his life was still going through some trials.

To put things into perspective, we can say that even today, our individual experience will be greatly influenced by the people with whom we have learned and continue to practice this Art. For many, it would be fair to say that 'you know what you know'. If you have only practiced aikido and have not studied weapons, your experience will be different from that of an aikidoka who has learned aikiken and aikijo from the Iwama Aikido school, for example, which is understandable. But are we right to say that this we are doing is still aikido or not?

Personally, I think that if the same aiki principles (the non-resistance, to keep it simple) are applied by an aikidoka who practices aikido without weapons, we should recognise aikido techniques and, yes, they practice the 'same' aikido too.

The same thinking applies to those who practice aikido and incorporate iaido or kenjutsu or jojutsu and will also have a different view from those who practice aikiken and aikijo from Iwama. In a nutshell, we are practicing the same aikido if the aiki principles are applied or if the techniques applied were done correctly and effectively. This, I think, truly expands our subject further and we can easily go beyond and debate what is an effective technique, if we want to.

To return to our main subject, however, do you believe in weapons or no-weapons practice?

I cannot speak for others but having studied Aikikai and Yoshinkan Aikido, I can say that the Iwama weapons system is a wonderful tool that builds your aikido and helps your taijutsu tremendously.

During pandemic, we could still practice aikido solo, doing our suburi training, which is a huge benefit, despite restrictions imposed by the government in order to maintain social distancing.

Bukiwaza training is not intended to be taught as a separate Art including aikiken or aikijo, unlike kenjutsu or iaido, while these are also fantastic Arts of their own. They have not been created to directly link with aikido. There are going to be some similarities, for sure, but they do not have the philosophy "think taijutsu when you practice iaido and vice versa", for instance. And that is why they are considered separate martial arts of their own.

In my opinion, the study of aikiken and aikijo is an essential element in building a solid foundation for the practice of taijutsu. Bukiwaza was never meant to be practiced more with ken and less with jo or vice versa, but to be studied 50/50, as each weapon is unique and offers many layers to reach a deeper understanding of our taijutsu.

When we practice bukiwaza, we think taijutsu and when we practice taijutsu, we think bukiwaza.

The study of bukiwaza offers precise footwork where we find many analogies between taijutsu and bukiwaza: like ken no kamae and kamae stance for katate dori, for example, with bukiwaza teaching the correct hip use, hip stability and solid posture, and how to build our kokyu feeling - all of which adds huge benefits to our taijutsu.

Kaizen creates a body development system which incorporates all aiki principles taught through the weapons practice, and that makes them so indispensable.

Here are some quotes that Stanley Pranin (RIP) shared from interviews he held with Morihiro Saito sensei:

Quotes from Morihiro Saito, 9th dan

"Before the war, the founder usually studied weapons by himself and did not teach these techniques to his students. It was during the Iwama period, mainly when only O-sensei and I were left, that he began to teach weapons...

"By the time I learned it, the 31-jo kata was already complete, but when Koichi Tohei sensei [presently head of Shinshin Toitsu Aikido] came to practice in Iwama it had not yet been perfected. What he learned was different from what I learned, probably because O-sensei's way of instructing was not yet fully developed.

"When I learned under O-sensei, his teachings included all of the weapons techniques including the kumitachi. At one stage, there was no one left in Iwama except me, so I trained with O-sensei by myself. His teaching gradually became more elaborate...

"The aikido that I learned consisted of both taijutsu and weapons techniques. We can use any type of weapon, but we mainly use the ken and jo. This is the only explanation I can give you.

"The founder explained aikido from many different viewpoints depending on the period and his state of mind. He said aikido was taijutsu that incorporated sword principles.

"So I believe aiki-ken and aiki-jo correspond to hanmi-ken and hanmi-jo. In other words, weapons techniques are expressed in the form of taijutsu, enabling you to enter into your opponent's space and throw him.

"The weapons-based techniques in taijutsu enable us to attack an opponent and throw him. I think taijutsu and weapons techniques should have a relationship, which is neither too close nor too remote.

"At the Iwama dojo I hold a weapons practice only once a week, so I am certainly putting the emphasis on taijutsu. But I think it is my duty, as one who was taught directly by the founder, to teach ken and jo to my students and to maintain the traditional teaching the founder left in Iwama."

It is fair to say that the Founder was a genius and a very talented martial artist but his way of teaching was difficult for many to truly understand. He often used a language that many failed to understand. During his lifetime, many instructors set their own aikido schools and explored with what they were given according to their 'own way and understanding' of the teachings of the Founder.

To name a few, talented martial artists such Gozo Shioda shihan with Yoshinkan Aikido, Kisshomaru Ueshiba, former Doshu, with Aikikai Aikido, Kenji Tomiki shihan with Tomiki Aikido, Koichi Tohei with Ki Society Aikido, Kazuo Chiba Shihan with Birankai Aikikai, Minoru Mochizuki shihan with Yoseikan Aikido, Morihiro Saito sensei with Iwama Ryu Aikido, all formed their schools and developed what we could see as their style of aikido.

Truly speaking though, the Founder never created any styles of aikido and so it would be right to think that there are no styles in aikido – aikido is aikido! This is why I believe in welcoming anyone who practices aikido, no matter which school they represent or are from and whether or not they practice weapons.

Primary Instinct and Aikido

Last night, after teaching our aikido session, one of our beginners asked me if aikido was really effective outside the dojo.

This is a question frequently asked by beginners and one that any teacher should not feel 'annoyed' when asked, as it is in my opinion a perfectly legitimate question!

I kindly responded to my student and explained that aikido has all the attributes and martial skills necessary to defend oneself. The process, however, take some time for us to absorb the techniques and understand aikido with its principles. I reiterated that the best form of self-defence is really to avoid getting into a difficult situation in the first place and I went on in more details.

If aikido training is done correctly in the dojo, an aikidoka should feel his primary instincts 'kicking in' during their training session. For instance, when you bow to your partner, do you do so at a close range with your partner? Do you look at your partner still when you do the bowing? If you do the above being too close and not looking at your partner when bowing, then you are 'simply trusting blindly' that your partner is never going to attack you. In my opinion, to practice in this manner in the dojo would be a mistake.

On the other hand, if you keep your distance from your partner when bowing (either in seiza or standing position), keeping eye contact with him, your partner will sense that you are 'ready' for the unexpected and will therefore not initiate since you are 'ready'. This kind of training quickly teaches you to be aware and 'listen' to your primary instinct.On the street, the rule of remaining vigilant applies, because any attacker first and always chooses his victim: he will pick those who are not aware or attentive to their surroundings or who look fragile and/or unsafe.

It is quite simple to understand: criminals will only attack if they feel they have the best chances to succeed, that is when their victims show these weak attributes.

I was told about a study done years ago by the Metropolitan Police. They hired a psychologist to interview a number of criminals behind bars who were specifically convicted for assault/theft/battery. They were shown a number of videos of pedestrians walking on the street and they were asked who they would choose to target and why.

It was revealed that all of them had said that they were only choosing victims who did not pay attention of their surrounding and/or looking weak or unconfident in the way they walked. 'It was their best chance to get what they wanted from their victims'.

So, if a potential victim is not showing these attributes, the attacker will simply wait for another target, pure and simple. If we walk outside feeling aware, we would be much safer to start with. To feel aware, however, you need to listen to your primary instinct.

If you sense you are feeling uncomfortable at some point outside your home, then this is your primary instinct telling you that something is wrong, so you should avoid this area or walking towards someone you think he may be up to no good. Sadly, most people ignore their primary instinct. We are living in a society that pre-conditions us that 'nothing should happen to you' when you go out.

Nobody expects to be attacked when you go to a supermarket or visit a coffee shop or when you go to your chemist and it would be right to think this too, but do not give in to such 'bait' that no one will ever come after you.

In the dojo, we do teach these things, focusing on kamae (stance), mae (distance), zanshin (alertness) and also using the correct etiquette with proper bowing, etc. I think that people forget that being aware of our surroundings is foremost what I would call a 'proactive' self-defence mode, and anyone can simply learn it very quickly!

Using aikido to defend yourself should **only** be the last resort. Avoiding getting into such situation is way better, to stay safe rather than getting into a potentially difficult and dangerous situation. "Prevention is better than cure" – this sentence is so true and applies to a lot of things in life.

If you have no other option to run away and you are cornered, then by all means use all you know thanks to your martial arts training to get out of this situation by defending yourself. You may even do so if you decide to stand your ground to defend your family or loved ones, when running away is not an option.

What is important to remember is this: even the best skilled martial artists can get seriously hurt – so be cautious and be safe. Use the proactive self-defence mode to avoid getting into such messy situation so that you can safely return home to be with your family and continue practicing aikido again and again...

Is Uke Opponent
or Partner in Aikido?

This question actually gives a hint about how different aikido is as a martial art compared to all others. For this reason, it deserves a chapter of its own to give you my honest answer and its motivations.

Before I do answer this interesting question, however, I think it is good to rewind to the very beginning first, and look at what really made you and I decide to join a martial art club: Many of us chose to learn a martial art to know how to defend ourselves and to be strong. These were my main reasons, by the way. Others joined a martial art club from an early age as children, so their parents introduced them to it. Others joined a martial art club because they fell in love with its discipline, its good etiquette forming strong values, the philosophy of respecting one another, etc.

When you took your first lesson in aikido, I am quite certain that you (as well as I) you thought uke was an opponent, someone you needed to defeat and overcome. Putting uke to the ground was the top priority and when it happened, it made you feel confident that you were on the path to learn how to defend yourself against a number of attacks. Well, I am giving you my honest thought, as I did think like this when I began!

However, I am imagining that at some point or perhaps rather quickly, your instructor began to show you the true meanings of aikido and how we must change our mindset from **opponent** to **partner** if we are serious in following its principles.

Needless to say, I was even more intrigued by this and it made me realise why the Founder kept saying aikido forms unity and peace, reconciling people together. I simply fell in love with aikido from that day onward and today I am still as eager as I was then.

This must have been an extraordinary finding for the Founder Morihei

95

Ueshiba to realise such things, because he had studied daito-ryu aiki jujutsu under Takeda Sokaku, who was a terrific martial artist and had a notorious reputation in Japan for being extremely skillful and one not to mess with! Like most Japanese martial arts, daito-ryu aiki jujutsu is a fairly ancient Art (in fact as old as 900 years old!). In this Art, uke is an opponent, therefore tori will have a mindset to eliminate the threat as quickly and efficiently as possible. You can imagine what happens to uke and all the possible pains he may be inflicted with.

Following his early studies of this Art, the Founder became affected by Japan's loss in WWII, which triggered something to change the Art with a view to reconcile rather than destroy. He transformed aiki jujutsu to aiki 'do': the way of the true warrior, which the Founder said should be 'to preserve peace and harmony, **not** to destroy it', so love is in the equation.

This concept, I think, really resonates with many aikidoka, hence why we practice this Art. Aikido gives me strength with an additional meaning in life, how we interact with one another with respect, which I find truly amazing. Some say that if everyone understood aikido and were practicing it, there would be peace on earth. I believe this too.

It comes as a true realisation that tori must be aware of how to see uke: no longer as an opponent but as a 'partner' in practice and in our lifetime journey in learning aikido. It is mostly tori that has to initiate and create this kind of relationship with uke. It is important to understand this.

As far as uke is concerned, he must carry on 'as before', i.e. being honest when delivering any attacks and to do so with vigour as well. Tori, on the other hand, must find a way to off-balance uke and subdue him **as a partner**. Ultimately, during practice we become gradually more caring towards our partner. We can increase the strength of our technique only if uke is ready for this.

Does it mean that we lose all martial concepts? Paradoxically, no. As far as uke is concerned, he remains in 'attacking mode', so to speak. Uke should retain his martial and budo spirit when attacking. Uke's attack should be **honest** and **real**, as it is the only way to retain a strong martial edge opposed to simply lose it altogether...

The concept of preserving peace is a very thin thread between retaining our martial etiquette or merely practicing gymnastics without any martial spirit.

Some may suggest that we should keep considering uke as an opponent and a partner at the same time, and I would also concur with this thought as long as the 'partner thinking' remains, so uke ultimately is still looked after!

It is 100% up to tori how to approach the situation and overcome uke, subdue the partner controlling his balance and using uke's momentum to redirect the force towards him with the use of kokyu, awase, correct posture, good hanmi and footwork, mae, triangle/square/circle/spiral movements, and to practice in the spirit of 'one against many', in order to achieve Takemusu Aiki when performing techniques.

I think that when we practice aikido it is very important that we bear a serious responsibility towards our partner whenever you are tori, executing the technique safely.

An advanced aikidoka should become a role model and set an example and lead the way to show what we mean by 'looking after' our uke. In turn, uke (who is an aikidoka) will grow feeling what we feel as tori and should be able to pass on our wisdom, love and this unique approach to any younger generations to come.

Aikido and Ego

When I began learning Aikido, I was just 16.

Being a teenager, I then thought that aikido could make me strong in order to defend myself, I learnt and copied the techniques dealing with various possible attacks (grips, strikes etc). I studied them and it became apparent that the more I was studying them, the more I came to realise that I needed to practice a lot more in order to know the techniques better and deeper.

Like in any class, the instructor would show us the technique from specific attack a few times and we would then have to quickly find a partner and practice the technique together taking turns being uke and tori. But by then there were some obvious obstacles: the instructor who demonstrated the technique made it look easy to do! The reality then hits you when realising that it is far from easy to do them!

The challenge of copying the technique correctly was one thing but there were far more obstacles, like your partner being bigger or stiffer or stronger or even awkward towards you. All of it really added some serious obstacles to my beginning. One thing is for sure, though: I was enjoying practicing aikido (even now and more so)!

But as I was determined to get there no matter how long it would take me. My determination was due to my hearing disability, having to prove to others that I could lead a normal life too. "You fall seven times and you get up eight times and carry on". This is exactly my testimony in my life, essentially due to my disability in my early childhood, as I wanted to show my mother that I deserved a place in a normal school instead of being in a school for disabled students, which crossed her mind at one point...

When you begin learning aikido and discover that the technique is not working as you would want it to, then you are naturally tempted to use your own strength to overcome your partner if he was making it more difficult with you. As you know, this is not how it is supposed to be done.

When you get to this stage, you use your own ego to overcome this challenge, because it gives you a quick answer to your problem. Who wants to be stuck? No one does, of course. So your ego (a voice in your head) tells you: "use your strength now". When you are a beginner, this may not be such a big deal but when you progress much further, you begin to be a lot more sensitive to this inner voice of yours and **you truly want to avoid that**.

Like all things, it truly does take a long time repeating the techniques and practicing them with different partners who are going to be smaller, taller, stiffer, bigger, stronger, more agile or supple. The truth is that you must experience the technique with as many partners as you possibly can, as it is the only way to know if your technique will work with everyone or not. It will tell also you if you are applying the technique correctly or not. If you practice with the same partners who may be sometimes too compliant, you may be in for a 'wake-up call' when you practice aikido with a different partner.

The fact that we can practice with all kinds of partners forges our aikido and help us to remove our ego in the process.

You have to be patient. This is a virtue that is not always seen, sadly. A good few practitioners decide to give up practicing because they realise it is too difficult or because they were on a very short journey to only pursue the black belt and then stop. This journey for just attaining the black belt is a trap, in my opinion, as those who follow it get seduced by their own ego. They believe that the level attained is 'enough' to be good in aikido and possibly to defend themselves outside the dojo.

For me, the journey to become shodan is only a beginning in pursuing deep learning of aikido.

Let's return to when I started practicing aikido: I was young and thought that by learning the 'physical' techniques, I would be then able to subdue and defend myself against any possible attackers. I suppose many of us have thought the same.

During my journey, it became clear that I misunderstood this bit, as truly it takes many, many years to master the techniques. Even though they are there to help us defend ourselves, the more I was practicing, the more I understood that I was not just learning to defend against any attackers but I was fighting with myself and my ego rather than against my partners.

You practice removing your ego and in aikido practice, a good teacher can be your guide to help you but ultimately can only show you the way: it is up to you to walk through the door or not.

In my case, if I was becoming stuck in a technique, I would try and find another way to reconnect with my partner or to simply accept what had happened and go back to basics, to rebuild my understanding. Your ego should not have a place to influence your learning of aikido.

Over the years, many aikidoka sadly have given up or stopped practicing aikido at some point, realising perhaps that it is a little bit more complicated than they had anticipated. Or due to a change of circumstances, they feel they do not need aikido anymore.

Whereas, there are some whom I regard as true warriors in spirit, as they continue to turn up to the dojo and keep practicing, week after week, month after month and eventually years after years. Some become teachers and teach good aikido spreading what they know and love about this Art and teach it humbly.

When you continue to learn aikido leaving your ego in a box, so to speak, I am confident that you will improve and begin to see deeper layers of what aikido truly is. We practice over and over again and our aikido gradually improves. When you do this constantly by seeking to enrich your technique, no matter what level you are, 3rd Kyu or 3rd Dan, you will find that the learning process will never end, as long as your ego is in put aside!

Sadly, there are some aikidoka who have been practicing for a number of years, and if we look at their aikido, we can notice that it appears to be 'stuck in time'. In another words, their aikido has not really changed over the years. I believe that this happens for a number of reasons: some simply stop pursuing the quest to improve their techniques believing that they have 'got it'. To me this would be a manifestation of their own ego that has blinded them and prevented them from progressing much further. Some simply just turn up to practice a little rather than seriously making constant improvement on their previous level of training.

In my view, if we are serious about wanting to improve our aikido, we must be honest with ourselves and be critical of our own aikido and therefore be mindful our own ego as well.

Is my ego at the forefront when I practice aikido or do I put it in a box when I practice aikido?

I know that truth hurts but we need to face it if we desire to be honest in wanting to attain a higher level in aikido. That is why I believe that if everyone on earth understood and were practicing aikido honestly, there would be peace on earth!

We don't just learn to fight but we learn to be in tune with our heart, and to connect with our partner, being in the awase that we often speak about in Iwama aikido.

My sincere advice to you reading this essay is to find a way to listen to your heart and trust your instincts toward aikido, enjoying every available moment as if it could be your last. I can assure you that the quality of your training will massively improve. Aikido has all the ingredients to make us better human beings, more respectful with one another.

The real question is "Are you willing to put your ego aside?" If you are, you will certainly be on a quest to gradually learn aikido on a whole new level, one never seen before.

Aspire Aikido London ›

Private group · 1.5K members

  Events

  View announcements   5

Approaching 1K Members of the Aspire Aikido London Facebook Group

Dear existing and new members,

It is wonderful to see that Aspire Aikido London Facebook group is now approaching 1K members (we might even surpass this number by the time this message is posted) - so I want to say thank you to everyone who has been a member to date for supporting Aspire Aikido London group and of course a big thank you to anyone new who is now joining us too!

I must admit that it feels quite amazing to see that we now have a pool of people who love aikido.

Truthfully, I find it encouraging to know that there is still a good group of people with the desire and passion to learn this wonderful Art, new generations and old generations alike, the second being the pillars for keeping our aikido alive: their teaching fires stimulates our inner "flame" to continue to burn within each of us, regardless of what happens to us and in the world we are currently living in.

From the bottom of my heart, I wish to thank all our senior instructors for doing what they do best, which is simply to keep practicing aikido daily, regardless of what is going on outside the dojo.

I think many will agree with me: "You are an inspiration to us all. You are in our heart for helping us directly or indirectly, when we watch you in person or on videos. You simply encourage us to do the same and to pursue our own personal journey in learning this wonderful Art! Domo arigato gozaimashita".

I do hope that so far you are finding our shared posts with videos/articles pleasant to watch/read and educational or even inspirational. We strive to share them from the bottom of our hearts and with a positive spirit where we can all appreciate one's Art in aikido even if we don't practice under the same school or teacher.

Sharing quality videos from other instructors is always enriching. We will continue to share Morihiro Saito sensei videos whenever we see any, as I think many of us see him as a source of inspiration for our personal quest in learning aikido.

Many will have watched Saito sensei's videos over and over again, appreciating his talent and exceptional skills, especially in being able to clearly explain to all of us how to progress and build our aikido to be strong.

We are indeed very lucky to be living in a digital world where we can find any of his videos by searching easily on YouTube or Google, something that could not have been done in the 1980's and 1990's, when they were available on VHS or DVD format only. Sadly, now that we have all the digital technology to support us, we are not seeing the large number of Aikido practitioners that we used to see in the 80s and 90s...

One could think that learning aikido would be more in demand thanks to the technology. Regrettably, it has drastically gone down prior to the pandemic and during it it has waned even further.

Is it because aikido is not giving what the younger generations are looking for? Or is it because aikido is failing to address what young people want to see? This certainly would bring a huge debate where everyone may have different opinions on how aikido should be and why it failed to attract young people in numbers.

I think that from reading my previous essays you will be aware that I am in favour of keeping aikido traditional and to pass this Art as faithfully as possible, keeping all the aiki principles in place: just what Morihiro Saito sensei did preserving O-sensei's aikido for us to appreciate what his aikido was. I believe there should be a solid interest with students who want to learn this Art.

My dream would be to 'revive' aikido, attracting the younger generations without having to change the Art. teaching it in such a way as to offer the younger generation a greater attraction to learn this art and, hopefully, to preserve it as a treasure for future generations who will benefit from both what this art means and from how it was intended to be taught.

The pandemic has been a difficult challenge for us all for the last two years and although it is not over, I feel we could be seeing the light at the end of the tunnel and the return to normality, as we are seeing more beginners joining now than before. Let's hope this continues!

Everyone is aware that the year 2022 has certainly been unprecedented, with everyone having to cope not only with Covid-19 but with the new international crisis caused by the war in Ukraine. Ultimately, this affects many people who may find it financially difficult to continue practicing aikido or to start learning this art because of inflation rising to the highest levels in a long time.

When there is a will, however, there is a way and I think people will find a way to continue, despite all odds. We have seen people returning to practice aikido in their clubs. We have shown our true resilience during the pandemic. People realised that even when we could not socialise, staying at home all day long, day after day, we always needed human contact for our well being. People have been missing the good hand shakes, the hugs, the affection exchanged with friends and family. I believe that we could be seeing a surge of people wanting to go out more than we did see over the past two years.

It has been said that aikido has all the attributes to help our well-being because it not only keeps our body fit and healthy, but also our mind and soul. Practicing aikido with one another, feeling physical contact, can be of great benefit and crucial to maintain and foster our well being and mental health.

I hope to see many of you when you join us in the amazing international seminar with Said Sebbagh Faa sensei, who will be visiting us in the UK this August 2022 for the first time. This seminar will be very inspirational, just like it was an amazing experience for me to meet Said Sebbagh Faa sensei in Spain. The training was so enriching that it gave me a much stronger flame to continue and I wholeheartedly wish the same to any of you in the pursuit of your own aikido study!

How to Practice Aikido

You may be wondering why I picked such a title for an essay, especially when it is implying how to practice your own aikido. Well, this is not about telling you how to do that from a technical point of view. I am only here to try and express how I have been feeling practicing my aikido for several years now and even more so since pandemic. That's when I started making and sharing my videos, hoping to support each other to stay positive and not give up aikido, since we couldn't have physical contact for quite a while...

For those who have been following my journey since becoming a member of the Aspire Aikido London group, and even following me before I re-launched Aspire Aikido London, you will have seen how relentlessly motivated I have been (and still am) and even more so when I re-launched the Aspire Aikido London Dojo in Hendon Central, London.

It is obvious to say that I could not have done any of that if I did not love aikido. Aikido is a part of me and my life and helps me to be stronger and accept who I am with my profound hearing disability. Because of aikido, I feel I can focus on life where work, family and aikido have their respective place.

I practice aikido with love and dedication, constantly striving to improve and research, all the while maintaining a beginner's mindset, day by day. All of this not only helps me progress in becoming a better person, but also helps me stay humble.

If anyone is serious about wanting to learn aikido - and the same applies for any other martial arts - you have to be aware that we are here to polish and forge our body, spirit and mind as one. This process makes us stronger individuals with a solid focus: better human beings.

I can speak for myself when I say that I have a 'burning flame' inside, or an inner voice that encourages me to do more and to continue. It may be called 'motivation' but I'd rather call it the 'burning flame' that one should keep going for as long as one possibly can – if the flame goes, so does your desire to improve - your motivation is gone as well.

You can keep the flame burning inside you even if you feel you have not got the technique right at any one point. I would call this 'determination': no matter what, you persist and continue to practice over and over again. To do this, however, you need that 'burning flame' inside you to stay on.

With this in mind, you will achieve the ability to fall eight times and get up nine – when you feel this, you are closer to being a true warrior. You simply will not give up – the only way is up.

Only your mind may tempt you to give up, not your body – remember this. Your body may be tired or broken, but if your mind is strongly determined you will still find the strength to get up, continue and do it again. Your mind forges your body and in turn your body forges your mind and spirit.

Here's another positive thing I would like to share. When you feel down about a technique, do not despair; on the contrary, rejoice this moment, as you are becoming aware of your errors – so you are moving up to a new level, and you will become aware of what to do to avoid making making the same mistake(s) next time...

When you feel not so great, focus on the positive sides of what you have and you will be instantly feeling much better and be more ready to try again. Why? Because your confidence will be with you to build your aikido further. To me that is how one should practice aikido and beyond aikido, live life. Easier said than done – I know.

When you practice in a dojo, the environment and the teacher should instigate positivity and a conducive atmosphere, which will help you feel good and happy to come in and practice again and again, without any ill intention from anyone who could hurt you.

If you practice in a dojo where you are thinking of quitting, then something could be wrong in the dojo itself. It may be that aikido is not for you but you may be surrounded by people who may not be supportive enough to make you want to continue practicing aikido. Aikido should make anyone feel great during and after any class.

When I joined Tony Sargeant's organisation (TIAE - Takemusu Iwama Aikido Europe), everyone made me feel truly welcome, like I was part of the family, and the kindness of everyone touched me right in my heart. At every aikido event I attended, Tony's partner, Jane, was absolutely wonderful (and she is a great cook, by the way, and has spoiled us all during our lunch breaks). I enjoyed meeting Nigel Porter sensei, Richard Small sensei, Kevin Haywood sensei, John Garmston sensei, Paul Weston sensei, Jenny Ousey sensei, Laurence Hobson sensei, Stuart Jeffs sensei, Alexander Gent sensei, Raj Soren sensei (apologies if I missed anyone), who were all amazing to meet collectively and individually. When you are in this kind of environment, you definitely want the day to be much longer so that we can practice, talk and share our passion for aikido and beyond.

More recently, I have flown to Spain to meet Said Sebbagh sensei and joined one of his aikido seminars. I was so excited about this trip and about meeting Said sensei and his close entourage, Tewfik Sebbagh sensei, Jose Manuel Barea Ramos sensei and a few of his senior students. I was immediately welcomed as part of their aikido family. It was truly magical.

Despite the language barrier, we were able to understand each other and we exchanged a great deal of knowledge. I was so excited and happy all the time! It was one of the best aikido seminars I ever attended.

It is truly amazing how aikido can unite people who practice peacefully. We bonded so nicely during the entire seminar that I was feeling really sad leaving the seminar on day 4: Said Sebbagh sensei delivered a sensational aikido seminar. I returned home, more on fire than when I left, with a strong desire to do more and to work on my personal aikido by adding the new things that I learned from Said Sebbagh sensei.

In my opinion that is how one should practice aikido: with a good heart, feeling happy and with a positive mindset, and always with fresh beginner's eyes, so as to be willing to change, to improve. Give up your ego and with determination, you will inevitably get one step further and higher even if it is a small step at a time. Better than none!

'Fail Big' in Your Aikido Practice...

I know it's quite a weird thing to say, if I am honest. However, I have been meditating on this for quite some time and I feel it is important to talk about failing in the dojo.

As a matter of fact, if we look at the bigger picture there is no such thing as failing, as making mistakes and learning from them is part of our learning process, if we are to build a stronger aikido.

We know that in aikido there is no 'competition' between partners. When we train in aikido there is no notion of choosing a winner and a loser at any time - which is something that attracted me to it in the first place. That's what I feel the need to talk about.

Unfortunately, we live in a society where we are taught to compete with one another, to be stronger than others. This mentality can be destructive and harmful toward our society as a whole, because it leads us to be more selfish. The only thing we care about is winning at all costs. It does not matter what the consequences are for our entourage or the environment, because the goal is to win, for example by achieving a certain financial profit goal. No consideration is given to the fact that achieving the goal could be extremely harmful to our peers, leading them to mental depression, or even worse that it could harm our environment through pollution - and the list goes on.

If we were all practicing aikido and this martial art was understood, I am convinced the world would be a better place. Aikido teaches us to be strong while supporting each other, not against each other: without rivalry. Failure is a part we must accept in order to learn to remain humble. In the dojo, it should not be something to be afraid of, quite the opposite – we must fail in order to understand what is wrong and from our mistake. We can then re-build, re-start and execute the correct movement. The word 'failure' is quite a stigma because of our upbringing in this society - but in aikido we learn to embrace it and deal with it, as it is the only way to become good. You have to fail first before you get it right.

No one was born a genius. Nobody in this world gets everything right the first time, no matter what that is. Those who have managed to be beyond anyone else are those who worked harder to achieve success. Let's look at any talented aikido instructor and consider how they do a certain technique: it is amazing! They simply worked hard to reach this level, and they too went through failures before getting that techniques right.

The 'Fail Big' in my title means exactly that: in the dojo, don't be afraid to get the movement or technique wrong. It is a place where you can make mistakes to perfect your technique, while your mind and spirit get forged too.

That said, it would be clearly wrong if you make the same mistake over and over again and refuse to change, despite your teachers' advice. Either you are having issues correcting a mistake, which sometimes could happen due to a technique being quite complex, or you are content with what you are doing and do not wish to make any additional improvements. In the second case you may have fallen into the ego trap.

Remember that when we practice aikido, we should do so with a beginner's mind, no matter what level in rank has anyone achieved. Ultimately, we are fighting with our own ego on a daily basis and until we die. Aikido is a great instrument to help you stay humble if you are truthful with yourself and wish to progress. The aikido body movements that we practice affect our spirit and mind and forge it for the better. We become better human beings when we remain humble and accept our mistakes.

Don't be afraid to make mistakes or don't be deflated. Fail in your techniques and understand what went wrong with your teacher's help, so that you can work on them and step by step become a better aikidoka.

Benefits of Ukemi in Aikido

Taking breakfalls in aikido is fundamental and remains an important process regardless of how far we progress in aikido. *Ukemi* will always be present in our daily practice.

Ukemi teaches us to get out of a fall safely thanks to forward and backward rolling. It should be mastered from the very beginning, if we really want to enjoy aikido and all the techniques it presents. The reality, however, is that no one really likes falling. If I am honest, we all prefer to be tori and do the technique than to be uke and receive it.

Why is that? Partly it is because of our upbringing, I suppose. We are taught from very young age to be the best, to win competitions, to rule and to be the strongest… therefore we all want to be the winners. We get praised when we are the winner. The loser is seen as someone who failed in his task or as failure altogether.

Thankfully, aikido gives us a new and more advanced viewpoint than just conquering or winning. We practice respecting one another, there is not a winner and a loser, we support each other. The Art is teaching us a new and more peaceful way to live together.

When uke falls, he is under extreme pressure and coping with it to retain his centre, despite being off balance. Uke is no longer losing but coping with the situation, in order to get out of it in the best possible way while avoiding being hurt.

When you see uke taking a beautiful breakfall, beginners' eyes may be amazed by tori doing the technique, but when you are fairly advanced, you will also appreciate the work of uke taking such a beautiful breakfall and you will respect uke for his ability to do that. Not just tori.

This bring to light what I think is magical about aikido: we respect both tori and uke, each for their part, as they both have a role to play that is equally and mutually important: neither is more important than the other. Tori is not the only one we truly appreciate. When a technique is performed from any specific attack, we do appreciate the work of both tori and uke.

On the street, if you were wearing a suit and tie, you would be very hesitant to do a breakfall. The dress code may hold you back, for a start, because you would probably not want to ruin your suit. You could fall awkwardly because your suit may give you limited mobility in your shoulders when you roll over. Also, you could hurt yourself if you do not know well enough how to fall. However, you may be amazed that if you were wearing a different attire, such as gym gear, or your gi, you may feel OK to try and do a breakfall.

After practicing for many years, I have experienced many breakfalls during training and surely get better over time. However, I have noticed that some aikidoka may feel more and more reluctant to take breakfalls, perhaps because of an injury, or simply because their age and fitness levels is making them stall and think twice before doing it. These are the ones who prefer to train in aikido as tori and put more emphasis in doing the technique than in receiving it.

When that happens, something is going to be missing to further your aikido. We all get older and it is important to look after our body by doing regular stretching and conditioning your body in a way that we can continue to enjoy aikido to its full, as it is meant to be. When you are taking the uke role, you are actually learning the technique more effectively, as I have already explained in one of my previous essays.

What I have also come to realise is that when you are receiving the technique, you are facing a challenge that you need to adapt to. You have to deal with the pressure, whether you are on your knees, or ready to roll over, and you do so by coping with the context you are subjected to. This is when you learn to handle the situation by maintaining your centre and zanshin at all times, and to discover where you should be positioned to best receive the technique and how to get out of the situation. In my opinion, ukemi is like the problems we face in life: how do you cope with the situations we meet? Do we give a 50% commitment and then change our mind? Or do we make a sound decision and commit 100% to what we have decided to do and accept its outcome? Or do we deal with the outcome as it happens, one step at a time, and live in the present moment? Ukemi really teaches us a lot about the struggles of life that we all face and fear.

Some may be afraid to fall but once they have the basics mastered, discover some form of confidence and accept that if the fall is inevitable, you have to embrace the moment and fall when the time is right.

Ukemi brings us to the very 'now' moment, and when you do fall, there is an instant, during the fall, where you are in a no-time zone, where there is no gravity either. It is difficult to explain but something builds inside you and you feel like you are being sucked into a timeless moment that is connected with you and your partner.

A good uke will sense how strong is the power being used by the partner and therefore how much power uke must engage in his own breakfall, whatever the type of it. The outcome will only depend on tori who is leading, but that can only happen when uke has the ability to receive normal and advanced breakfalls.

Ukemi has to be done without fear and having the body in tune with its centre, so you are feeling relaxed and yet alert to that very moment in which the fall happens.

Uke should not strike to prevent the fall from occurring. When uke attacks, he should do so because he believes that he can get tori, which gives tori a better opportunity to get his technique and awase right.

In Iwama Aikido, we often begin with kihon. Uke begins with a strong attack and tori is in the worst possible starting point. This type of training is done to help tori find the technique without using an excessive amount of strength to subdue uke. In fact, when the technique is executed correctly, there is little effort from tori, but there is only one specific way to do this. When kihon is practiced in that manner, both tori and uke can benefit 100% of the exchange, and it becomes possible to begin the awase training, which adds a new challenge. Uke should still attack as if he believes he can quickly control the situation. Tori has to blend in well with the attack: too soon, uke can redirect and strike again; too late and uke will succeed hitting tori. The right blending happens when uke is fully committed to his attack and it would be impossible to change it. It is at this point that tori must blend and draw the power away from uke to carry out his *nage* technique.

If uke ends to the ground, when getting up many tend to switch off their zanshin. This is a mistake: uke should remain connected with tori thanks to zanshin towards tori both when going down and getting up. Zanshin should never be turned on and off; it should be on all the time. This allows tori to train better, as he can sense a superior presence and that helps him maintain his zanshin.

Ukemi does not mean you are 'losing' but that you are coping rather well under such an extreme condition and that you have a plan to cope under this extreme condition. When you understand ukemi, you will apply this thinking outside the dojo, in your workplace and wherever you are facing the various challenges that come your way. Thanks to aikido training, you will gain greater confidence in your physical ability, and this in turn will boost your mental strength in coping with pressure in life.

Aikido has so many attributes to help you and help others. It has given me the ability to fight back not only against other people but to fight back against my own doubts and fears. When you conquer ukemi, you definitely feel much stronger, more confident in yourself. In my case, it gave me the confidence I could do things just like anyone else, despite my profound hearing disability. Aikido has its own ways to build your body and forge your mind: ukemi is one of its magical tools to transform each of us into something stronger.

Is Aikido Lacking Tangible Attacks?

The fact that I am starting my writing with this question may make you guess that I actually agree with the question asked. The answer is actually both 'Yes' and 'No'.

Allow me to elaborate, starting with the 'Yes' answer. Aikido lacks tangible attacks when we see that uke is not putting 100% commitment behind any attack. In doing this, uke holds back his attack because he is focusing on what is about to happen next step, for example a throw, or a pinning technique. Without realising, uke anxious about the next step and simply omits delivering a strong attack in the first place.

The result of this has a devastating effect on convincing people that aikido is effective as a whole, after they have witnessed an exchange based on the above premises. Anyone who sees this for the first time, both untrained or experts in martial arts, will agree that there is no way it would work in reality.

They will surely tell you that uke is complying too much or that uke delivered a poor attack. This makes tori look like he could only manage the situation because the attack was weak in the first place. Some may even argue that when faced with a strong attack tori would struggle to get past the first attack, before attempting any technique...

It's hard not to concur with these views when uke is delivering a poor attack or simply giving tori their arm(s) fort the technique to be done. We often see that uke is fully complying, instead of trying to resist and counterattack tori, especially when uke's balance is unaffected.

Having said this, however, I remain convinced that aikido is actually not lacking any tangible attacks at all - **if uke is attacking correctly**. As a matter of fact, uke can control tori right from the start, by grabbing well, for instance.

If you bring a strong attack from the start as uke, you can build confidence as an attacker that is capable to take the initiative. As tori, you have to apply the technique correctly to subdue your partner, no matter what attack is delivered to you, be it a hold or a strike. Tori also needs to apply the right timing and use his hips to affect uke's balance from start to finish - the last element being, in my view, essential to make aikido powerful.

When we practice as I just described, I can confidently say that aikido is very strong from both uke and tori sides. We also need to step back and accept that we are all learners and it will be inevitable to make mistakes along the way during practice and repetitions, class after class, year after year.

What is important is to retain the basic principle of attacking well and of doing the technique correctly, using the hips and checking if uke's balance is affected or not. It would be a waste of time to successfully take uke's balance at the beginning and then allow uke to regain it half way through. The moment uke gets back on his feet, you would have done the first part of the technique in vain. The technique must be done in a way that uke cannot retaliate from start to finish.

Years ago, a friend of mine who is a Shotokan Karate instructor taught me a very important lesson. I have digested each of his words and applied them in aikido: "You can be the best fighter in the whole world and be able to punch extremely fast, but if your balance is taken, you cannot fight back. Why? Because when we lose our balance our brain is not allowing us to fight back."

If you apply aikido keeping your partner's balance under control from start to finish, you will have the most powerful technique. I am convinced about that.

One of the keys is to fully concentrate on the **now** moment, without thinking of the **future,** what will happen next, or the **past** (Did I move correctly? Are my feet in the correct position? etc).

The right approach would be for uke to fully attack and for tori to move with the right timing, when uke cannot alter the direction of the attack as his commitment is engaged. This is very difficult to do and to achieve this level of technical ability requires years of practice for both uke and tori.

What we should not see is uke failing to attack and instead giving away their arms(s) to tori to easily execute techniques. If the attack is a *tsuki*, the tsuki should be executed with good hip power and with good body posture. The same applies to *shomen uchi* or *yokomen uchi:* uke should bring these attacks using good hip power, being relaxed and without sending a 'telegram' beforehand, i.e. making the attack obvious and visible from a mile away. In the real world, no attacker would behave like this. The attacker would only commit to a certain attack knowing he has a chance to succeed with it.

Another common issue is that tori seems to be committed only to one specific attack and therefore moves in full confidence that uke will fully comply with this expected attack. If uke has not yet committed to any attack and you move in too early, uke can change the attack at the last moment and tori could be in a vulnerable position for a split second. It may be too late after that...

In my opinion, this should never be happening. Tori should be positioned in a specific kamae that invites uke to attack in a specific way. In Iwama aikido, we are taught to apply different kamae stances that may influence uke to attack in a certain way, rather than blindly go for any attack of his choice – for instance, if we stand in hitoemi kamae position, we tempt uke to strike yokomen uchi, or grab *kata dori* or strike *mawashi geri.* Our hitoemi is giving limited options to uke in terms of available attacks uke can bring. This is due to the positioning of our body, that would make it difficult to attack with *ryote kata dori, men uchi,* or *tsuki,* for example.

When we understand the various kamae and the options they offer to uke, we realise that it is tori that creates a 'bait', so to speak, where tori is leading the way from start.

Therefore, it would be incorrect to think that tori is only reacting to uke initiating the attack. The attack is happening because tori has given 'an opening', tempting uke to grasp this opportunity. For this reason, I would add that aikido is far more on the offensive side than a self-defense Art. Tori is 'ahead' of uke in his mind process. This is important to understand.

As uke, you must make sure to give tori a good and as real an attack as possible. Thanks to that tori can can work on his mae, body posture, footwork, body movement, awase. He can learn to feel from the hara when moving and connecting with uke. He can study how to apply the technique as it is meant to be done, with strong kokyu but keeping the body relaxed, the mind being 'empty' and alert to the 'now' moment.

It sounds easy but it is not. It takes years and years of practice, repeating these movements. What is important is not to fall into robotisation mode, where we do the techniques using our body but without any inner feelings.

Inner feelings must begin before the physical movements. We should always apply the technique thinking that uke could succeed in his attack, thus giving uke the impression he can succeed, then blending in with the right timing to subdue uke and be immediately ready for next attacker...

In terms of positioning, tori should always act as if surrounded by multiple attackers, ready to move away from a potential threat. Avoid doing 'one on one' aikido. To be able to do this, tori must have a steady and calm mind surrendering the past and future to the 'now' moment only, embracing the 'life and death' scenario.

Considering all the above points, you will agree that aikido has all the attributes to offer strong tangible attacks from the uke side. It can also offer solid techniques from the tori side to subdue uke's attacks and to manage multiple attackers at once.

Aikido techniques are wonderful for developing our physical and inner strength, but there must be a process for absorbing what is being demonstrated, copying what the instructor is showing, and repeating it. We all make mistakes and through the process we can learn what to do to avoid being in this situation.

Therefore, you can appreciate why aikido takes a long while before we notice a significant transformation. Aikido is a lifetime study but one that is truly worth it!

Aikido and Mind Training

Whenever you go to the gym, you may have set a goal or objective for yourself, such as to gain muscle mass and/or lose weight or simply to exercise regularly for your own well-being or for any other reason.

Whatever reason motivated you, your mind played a role in your decision to train for the purpose of transforming your body and feeling better about yourself.

When you go to the gym, your mind influences you, choosing the exercises to do and telling you when you should push yourself to do a little more or not to quit. At some point, your mind may even tempt you to stop or quit altogether - this is true of exercise at the gym or any other activity.

Overall, this is the way your mind works in relation to the sports activities you have undertaken. It will be there to motivate you, for example in continuing to do what you are doing in the gym. Therefore, training can be considered as a physical activity with a good amount of mental focus to help you achieve your goals.

Most people will begin their training with a simple mind focus, maybe to lose weight. When they see that to shed pounds is far from easy, after trying for a while they will be tempted to quit. When you get to this point, you may have reached substantial reasons why to quit: perhaps the physical activity may be too repetitive and boring, but I would say that the mind is not focused enough to continue regardless.

In my opinion, to last for a long time you need to be in love with what you do. To be able to practice aikido without giving up, one must have a strong desire to learn the art and, at some point, fall in love with it.

If a person's goal is to reach black belt, then very often this person will abandon aikido when this goal is reached, because the mindset has been set within a set limit. Becoming shodan means becoming a true beginner, now ready to discover aikido much further and at a deeper level.

The key for not giving up is how much you really want it. How driven are you to get there? Are you only focused on one target? If you only hold a limited motivation or a small mind focus, your long-term commitment will not work.

I am not here to deny the value of training in the gym, because it bring lots of good things too. However, it does not explore our mind deep enough compared to what aikido (and martial arts as well, to be fair) can do.

In aikido we talk openly about our mind and explore it much more deeply. We end up discovering ourselves and find out when our mind and body are at their highest level. In other words, we explore our limits in terms of strength and weakness.

If we practice aikido the way we brush our teeth, daily, and accept it as a lifetime study, then we will eventually explore this Art much further and much deeper both at physical and mental level. In aikido we explore what our mindset should be during stillness and movement.

At first, the mental process will be the same as explained in relation to going to the gym. Through desire, your mind will convince you that this is what I want to do, "I want to learn aikido." It may be because you watched an aikido demonstration live or on video, or because you want to learn how to defend yourself. Or perhaps you feel you want to explore the spiritual side that aikido can offer, or simply want to do a physical activity that is not what you get in the gym and want to train with a partner rather than being alone.

In aikido we learn to make our bodies flexible, agile and capable of dealing with attack. However, aikido offers another kind of practice besides the physical: it provides a 'gym for the mind', synchronised with body posture (stillness) and body movement (action). The more I practice aikido, the more I realise that I am exercising my mind over my body.

When you do that, after a session you will feel exhausted mentally, because you have been deeply focusing your mind with your body. I would like to point out that the spirit plays an important part as well, by linking your 'heart', or good soul, to all you do - both during practice and outside practice.

This mind focus I am referring to takes place thanks to zanshin, which is to be maintained throughout the technique. The mind focus also extends to mind readiness: being ready, with an empty mind, i.e. thinking of nothing but feeling you are part of the **now** moment, being present, being alive, being ready for what may come. One surrenders and accept that life and death can be close but you are 'victorious' because you choose the former, to be here.

I used to feel this level of awareness called zanshin when I worked as a door supervisor in night clubs. My constant awareness, watching my back, has led me to feel more conscious of my surroundings and the people around me. At the end of my shift, I felt really tired and every night I worked I had to keep my zanshin when walking on the street to get home. It was needed to keep me safe and alive. Had I not practiced aikido, I probably would not have had the same mindset. Aikido teaches you to explore its core principles with our mind and body, taking them outside the dojo. Zanshin stayed with me outside the dojo and helped me tremendously during my career as door supervisor and beyond.

The aikido etiquette we learn in the dojo also brings the right messages to discipline our mind and body. During the practice, we quickly learn to be ready and to live in the 'now' moment. This can only be done if we discipline our mind to avoid overthinking. Looking at your feet, correcting the position you are in, repeating a movement during the execution of the technique: we think that aikido lies its the physical forms, but it actually lies in the mind first before the body. The mind has the ability to be distracted or be totally focused in whatever you do.

When you do your bowing, if your mind is clear and empty, the physical gesture will reflect your mindset. In another words, the act of bowing is much deeper than physical motion of bowing. The same applies with all aikido techniques.

Since aikido involves many circular and spiral movements, these actions will also positively affect our mind. We develop sensitivity to our partner and surroundings, but this sensitivity increases in our mind, which is influenced by the body shapes and movements in which we have been involved as tori and uke.

I suppose that this is where we can say that aikido is magic in a sense, because the physical techniques have somehow a deep effect on us, an effect on our mind that will gradually make us better human beings, more compassionate towards another.

To be 100% focused, we must empty our mind and be present in the 'now' moment, so that we are fully receptive to what is happening. When we do this and feel the technique through emptiness, it is our body that becomes much more receptive, not our brain. Our body or the skin is our second 'brain'. The body takes over and will react according to what is happening, so we do not intellectually think from our main brain.

To understand it, however, takes quite some time. What I just wrote may sound odd to a beginner, but when you practice regularly for a period of time, you eventually understand how the second brain works.

There is a deeper level within zanshin, which is to maintain awareness of tori and uke both and more so on uke when receiving a nage or a pinning technique. When we get up, our mind must remain vigilant and feel the connection with our partner through zanshin and correct *maai*.

When we get stuck with a technique, we also need to teach our mind to avoid resistance or avoid listening to our ego, that will be tempting us to exert more strength to 'make the technique work'. Focusing on developing the right mindset is also a good tool for becoming more humble.

The blending part, known in Iwama Aikido as awase is quite a challenge for beginner and intermediate practitioners, as it takes a lot of discipline to move in at the right time, not too early or not too late. We blend in at the very moment when uke is fully committed to an attack. In effect, there is no concept of action and reaction or block and attack. With the awase/blending concept, Aikido presents something deeper - a synchronous equilibrium with uke that makes our reciprocal attacks bring tori into uke's central line in one move, avoiding the block-and-attack strategy that would amount to two moves.

Studying awase requires a specific state of mind: one must achieve complete emptiness so that your mind and body is fully receptive to what may happen next and to be present in the 'now' moment. Very difficult to do, it requires great mental concentration to be ready to move in at any time but only when uke has initiated.

There is then the question of maintaining uke's balance under control from start to finish, while avoiding being only focused on your partner. Our mind must be focused much further than our partner: you need to be ready to handle any other potential or additional threat. In our training, we focus on being alone but surrounded by multiple attackers both in all taijutsu techniques and bukiwaza as well. Bukiwaza practice truly opens your eyes in relation to being surrounded by multiple attackers, and in turn we carry this principle with us when we practice taijutsu with the mind focus that I described above.

For example, if we pick the technique tai no henko, with a partner holding our hand, it is actually not a technique designed to be used 'one on one', i.e. focusing on subduing the partner who is holding our hand. In doing so, our mind would only be focused towards our partner, which is not getting you ready against multiple attackers. Tai no henko is actually a technique designed to show you the principle of being surrounded. We focus our mind that the threat is not with our partner holding us but with what may happen behind us that we cannot see. When we focus on turning in the opposite direction, or same side as our partner, we widen our awareness to a full 360 degrees. The fact that we have been focusing on something other than our partner grasping our hand makes it easier and without too much effort to overcome uke's grasp - if good body posture is applied, with good kokyu, proper footwork and rotation with the hips.

When we discover this different mindset, we put our trust in the techniques and adopt our mind in relating to the technique. That is why aikido cannot be merely a physical movement in which techniques are copied without the mind focusing on technique.

The technique becomes alive and sharp when body, mind and spirit are involved, and this makes aikido powerful. We want our mind to be empty, our body to be relaxed, our spirit to be connected with our heart. These three ingredients together create big impact in the techniques, whereas they are not enough on their own. To perform strong aikido, we deploy these three ingredients and add the aiki principles that aikido has 'in its sleeves'.

Once we do this, we enter a whole new level in which we continually discover new things within the techniques we thought we knew. It is a constant discovery or improvement that seems to be never-ending. Aikido has its way to reveal much more to us when we have the right mindset and experience. That is the secret that aikido unveils when you are ready technically and with the right mindset.

In truth, the more we practice, the more we feel the need to learn, once new things are understood or revealed. Often these discoveries are in the small details but they make a huge differences for our aikido.

All of these may be revealed to you if you have the right mindset and spirit, that is if you are a good humble person. Let go of your own ego and adopt the right mindsets and aikido will reveal itself to you, step by step, for good…

Internal Feeling with Aikido

This is perhaps a difficult topic to discuss here because it relates to inner feelings and manifests a certain state of mind that is often a challenge to describe in words. I will try to talk about it as clearly as possible by sharing my personal experience, which of course I am not claiming is the only way to experience inner feelings in aikido.

After practicing for the past 32 years, I have realised that when you are doing aikido, there is something that works deep inside, once you function with a very specific mindset: a calm, goodhearted mindset with an empty mind - all these elements working together.

When you mention 'internal feeling' to beginners, it will simply mean absolutely nothing to them. A new practitioner will concentrate on copying the external forms of what appears to be with any specific techniques we demonstrate, which is absolutely fine and normal, as we all started there too. Talking about internal feeling with beginners will be pointless. What one should point in their case is how to use the hips to execute a certain movement, for example, and that explanation will be of help in the long run.

After years of practicing aikido (it may take 10 years or more), if you do not feel any inner sensation or get any feeling from your hara, you should perhaps question how you should practice in the foreseeable future. Aikido is much more than the mere execution of physical aikido techniques.

The key lies with being honest with yourself. We need to be open and critical regarding our aikido, which will help guide us in what we need to do to work on finding this inner feeling or sensation. If you adopt the kaizen approach (see relative chapter), you will surely be on the right path to question where you are in your own personal aikido journey.

In my own experience, the discovery of internal feeling has begun with the study of *ken suburi,* and in particular with the 1st ken suburi.

In the 1st ken suburi, you begin by executing your cuts in a physical manner, just as any beginner would. Gradually, however, you start looking for alternative ways to cut avoiding the use of shoulders and arms, simply because it starts to hurt when you are doing the same cuts over and over again.

Your teacher will suggest you to "relax your shoulders and arms and to cut from the hara (centre)". You hear this sentence and at first you will not be sure what this means. So you keep on doing what you think you can do at your own pace. Proper footwork must be maintained throughout the cut and you quickly realise that it is more complicated than you thought.

You need to cut and maintain the correct footwork during the whole cut and back into ken no kamae. Thus, you work on the physical form for a while and try and figure out how to do the cut and footwork correctly but you gradually begin to see that you need to link the cut and the footwork movement together. You try and do this at the same time and you find that you are not in the right pace with the upper and lower body. Both are working on their own.

You observe your teacher, or you may check Morihiro Saito sensei's videos and notice 'how clean and simple' their movements appear to be when they cut. They cut and move in perfect harmonisation, at the same time, all as 'one move', with cut and footwork happening together.

To share my personal experience again, I became intrigued with understanding this part of cutting as one move. I kept (and continue to keep) a beginner's mind and knew that there had to be something more than just the cut and the footwork to be able to make the cut with the feet and arms moving together. And I looked deeper, trying to find a relaxed cut with legs and upper body synchronised and functioning as one move.

The more I was able to relax the more I could feel my movements eventually emerging from hips (and also known as centre or hara). It started small but with confidence and with repetition, I began to understand better my hips movement, such as pulling my right hip to bring the ken upward, and to bring my front right leg back towards my left foot. Then when I cut down doing the 1st ken suburi, I pushed back my right hip forward and pulled my left hip to the side during the final cut.

In my opinion, the 1st ken suburi is the hardest technique in aikido and it also represents the 'heart' of all aikido techniques. All movements we do begin with hips moving similarly to the 1st ken cut - a ken cut that looks so simple in itself but yet is so hard to do, as it is so detailed in its simplicity, and requires to be done exactly as it is supposed to, no more no less.

For this reason, the 1st ken suburi will take years of repetition and constant dedication and perseverance to master. One must adopt the right mindset I described earlier as well. On the other hand, when you begin to feel what this cut is meant to be, the reward is immense: an inner sensation/feeling begins to take place.

When you discover such feeling, then you begin to realise more and more that the cut is not done by the mere arms lifting the ken, with right leg moving on its own: both of these are done with your hips. Your hips become the command centre for all movements that are about to happen. This also applies for the whole of aikido too.

If you remove the ken from your hands, you should still have the same hips feeling in taijutsu. If you choose tai no henko, this technique should be no different from 1st ken suburi done with the hips - **not** with the arms and legs moving separately.

An advanced aikidoka will actually notice if an aikidoka is using his hips or not when doing the techniques. An advanced aikidoka will also notice when another practitioner has found the inner feeling we have described - something that profoundly changes their understanding and allows their eyes to see everything differently from any beginner.

This also brings the subject of whether or not one should be learning weapons that I wrote about in my previous essay *Weapons or no weapons in aikido.* I am convinced that learning our weapons system will help you find this inner feeling.

An aikidoka who does not study weapons may find it hard to perceive such feeling, and could be continuing with what I called a mere physical aikido, with techniques that lack inner feeling. Aikido techniques must be done with strong inner feeling and connection with partner: connecting with the partner as one, blending with awase, moving without struggling, relying on the hips rather than the shoulders and biceps to carry out the movement.

The hips are the largest joints in our body. There is a good reason why we should use them rather than our smaller joints, such as the shoulders.

When we use the power of the hips, we can defeat anyone, regardless of their size. Our founder Morihei Ueshiba was only five feet two tall and was able to overcome multiple attackers simultaneously and with ease. He was truly extraordinary in the use of hip power.

The more relaxed we are, the more connected we become with our hips, and this is where our first awase begins, with our body synchronising our hips with our lower and upper body.

Our strong practice method, based on learning to connect with our partner starting with kihon practice and then moving on to ki no nagare, is designed to help build hip feeling in aikido.

Awase is an essential component that is involved in all our techniques, both kihon and ki no nagare. We seek a strong connection with the partner, but this starts with our hips - before we overcome any partner.

There are, of course, many other elements to add to our aikido training. One of these that I would like to emphasise is the rhythm that the tori must keep. Whether we are training in kihon or ki no nagare, our rhythm must be in tempo: just like a beat in music, we must stay in tune with our hips and our connection with our partner.

The inner feeling will eventually be strengthened and we will be able to perceive the inner feelings of the triangle, square, circle and spiral, which will be manifested internally in our hara and externally with the expression of aikido techniques, both of which work together forever...

About
Nicolas (Nick) Regnier

I was born in 1972 in France, where I grew up in Nantes, historically part of Brittany. I grew up in a typical French family, surrounded by love and stability. When I was in France, I was lucky enough to be with my parents and grandparents. I also have two great younger brothers, Ludovic and Johann Regnier, who I know admire my path and the way I deal with my profound hearing disability.

My interests in martial arts truly began in 1987-1988, when I discovered aikido under strong recommendation from a kung fu master I met in Nantes.

In 1988 I turned 16 and embarked on hospitality studies in St Nazaire. I attended five days a week and returned to Nantes every Friday night, then returned to St Nazaire on Sunday evening.

I began studying Aikikai Aikido under the FFAAB in 1988 and enrolled in Aikido classes in both Nantes and St Nazaire. In 1990, I relocated to Nantes to further my hospitality studies and I joined the FFAAA, studying Aikikai Aikido under Philippe Gouttard shihan. In 1991 I embarked on my journey to London and studied Aikikai Aikido with Minoru Kanetsuka Sensei.

In 1993 I took a door supervision course to get my Westminster Council license, and that,s when I met David Rubens shihan, who was the instructor for the door supervision course. In 1993 I started practicing Yoshinkan Aikido at the Meidokan Yoshinkan Aikido Dojo in West Hampstead. From 1993, I worked as Licensed Door Supervisor in various notorious night clubs in West End area of London

In summer 1995, I joined The London Aikido Club under Dojo-cho Andy Hathaway sensei and began my journey studying Iwama Aikido.

In 1995 I left my job as door supervisor at the Sports Café to work as security officer at the Regents Palace Hotel in Piccadilly. In 1998 I joined the Mayfair Intercontinental Hotel as a security officer and was later promoted to security manager. In 2001 I moved as security officer to the Churchill Intercontinental Hotel (now known as Hyatt Regency London - The Churchill).

In 2003, I joined Gallowglass Security Company as a training manager and security events manager. In 2005, I established my own company, Cledor, a leading provider of on-site property staffing services in London and the Southeast. To date, I run and manage my company with over 120 employees, assisting many block managers and real estate developers with our tailored on-site staffing services, ranging from concierge, housekeeping, concierge, security, to building managers, estate managers, etc.

In 2012, I launched the Aspire Aikido London Dojo in Harrow, London, where I teach on a weekly basis.

Acknowledgments

This book is here thanks to all my Teachers who inspired me to continue learning, aikido.

A special thank to:

Philippe Gouttard shihan

Minoru Kanetsuka sensei (RIP)

David Rubens shihan

Andy Hathaway sensei

Tony Sargeant sensei

Said Sebbagh sensei

I also want to thank my family, starting with my parents, my father André Régnier and my mother Marie-France Régnier, and my two younger brothers Ludovic and Johann Regnier, for their love and support despite the geographical distance.

I wish to thank my wife, who is my rock and the love of my life and who supports me in everything I do, especially in Aikido. I am blessed with two beautiful children, whom I love deeply. I would like to thank my sister-in-law, who has always been by our side whenever we have needed extra support with family and beyond!

I thank my students who practice with us at Aspire Aikido London Dojo and especially Jermaine Clarke, Maciek and Magda Bo who kindly agreed to participate in the photo shoots.

I thank Stephanie Belton, a very talented photographer, who made our photos look superb for our website and for this book! And of course I thank Line Bjørhovd who has been outstanding in designing our website and handling all the new content when requested.

I thank all the members of TIAE (Takemusu Iwama Aikido Europe):

Nigel Porter sensei, Richard Small sensei, Richard Thomson sensei, Paul Lowing sensei, Peter Reynolds sensei, John Garmston sensei, Jenny Ousey sensei, Laurence Hobson sensei, Kevin Haywood sensei, Mark Berry sensei, David Partington sensei, Paul Weston sensei, Noela Bingham sensei, Alexander Gent sensei and Raj Soren sensei for accepting me and making me feel so welcome in this wonderful family community.

Finally, as his message is very special to me, I would like to thank Tony Sargeant sensei for believing in me and giving me all the unwavering support I needed to relaunch Aspire Aikido London. Truly, without his help it would have been difficult to do so.

André Cognard: Living Without Enemy
The Ran Network- The Budo Classics #1
Buy it now: https://www.amazon.com/dp/B09Y5VWHMX

In this philosophical essay steeped in body practice, Aikido teacher André Cognard discusses Eastern traditional martial arts by exploring his own history, perceptions and emotions.

Cognard dwells in particular on the areas concerning the relationship with others and the conflicts that inevitably arise with them. In a direct and effective way, the author does not present us with "the object of a sudden revelation, but rather the fruit of a slow evolutionary process due to a laborious, humble practice, studded with failed attempts and repeated with a doggedness that sometimes defies reason".

André Cognard tells us that "Living Without Enemy" is possible and that the way to reach such a state through martial arts is through the awareness that they have evolved and continue to do so.

André Cognard analyses conflict, present and past violence, the inner enemy, bodily identity, friends, enemies, and hatred. Explaining the pivotal words in martial arts, he offers us a decalogue for learning to serve and be free, to respect, acknowledge, accept, thank and love.

The author explains how essential is the concept of transforming energies within oneself: anger, anxiety, fear can indeed be fully mastered and lead to new and potentially enriching circumstances. It is therefore necessary to know how to work on oneself: this book effectively shows how to manage our fears of the unknown. Because our first enemy is within ourselves!

The Aiki Dialogues

The Aiki Dialogues present some of the most established voices in the world of Budo and Aikido while giving space to the most interesting emerging characters of the martial community

Find purchase links: https://aikidoitalianetworkpublishing.com/the-aiki-dialogues/

#1 - The Phenomenologist - Interview with Ellis Amdur
#2 - The Translator - Interview with Christopher Li
#3 - The Wrestler - Interview with Rionne "Fujiwara" McAvoy
#4 - The Traveler – Find Your Way - Interview with William T. Gillespie
#5 - Inryoku – The Attractive Force - Interview with Gérard Blaize
#6 - The Philosopher - Interview with André Cognard
#7 - The Hermeticist - Interview with Paolo N. Corallini
#8 - The Heir - Interview with Hiroo Mochizuki
#9 - The Parent - Interview with Simone Chierchini
#10 - The Sensei - About Yoji Fujimoto
#11 - The Teacher - Interview with Lia Suzuki
#12 - The Innovator - Interview with John Bailey
#13 - The Uchideshi - Interview with Jacques Payet
#14 - The Body-Mind Educator - Interview with Paul Linden

The Ran Network full catalogue:
https://therannetwork.com

Printed in Great Britain
by Amazon